PRAISE F

ELEVATING FUTURES

"Dr. Tracee Perryman's style and extraordinary technique effectively tie student motivation to relationship building, classroom culture, and metacognition. This book encompasses the Afrocentric Responsive Classroom for K-3 educators and, if used correctly, can advance instruction of essential academics, social justice practices, routines, and behaviors for African American children alongside students of all ethnic backgrounds. To conclude, the author uses practical advice that builds upon best practices that educators already integrate in their classrooms and familiarizes us with the intentional usages of interactive modeling theories throughout all educational learning communities. Superb!"

—Dr. James M. Jones, Principal, Toledo Public Schools

ELEVATING FUTURES

TRACEE PERRYMAN, PHD

ELEVATING FUTURES

A MODEL FOR EMPOWERING BLACK ELEMENTARY STUDENT SUCCESS

Advantage.

Published by Advantage, Charleston, South Carolina.
Member of Advantage Media Group.

ADVANTAGE is a registered trademark, and the Advantage colophon is a trademark of Advantage Media Group, Inc.

Printed in the United States of America.

10 9 8 7 6 5 4 3 2 1

ISBN: 978-1-64225-299-6
LCCN: 2021923719

Cover design by David Taylor.
Layout design by Wesley Strickland.

This publication is designed to provide accurate and authoritative information in regard to the subject matter covered. It is sold with the understanding that the publisher is not engaged in rendering legal, accounting, or other professional services. If legal advice or other expert assistance is required, the services of a competent professional person should be sought.

Advantage Media Group is proud to be a part of the Tree Neutral® program. Tree Neutral offsets the number of trees consumed in the production and printing of this book by taking proactive steps such as planting trees in direct proportion to the number of trees used to print books. To learn more about Tree Neutral, please visit www.treeneutral.com.

Advantage Media Group is a publisher of business, self-improvement, and professional development books and online learning. We help entrepreneurs, business leaders, and professionals share their Stories, Passion, and Knowledge to help others Learn & Grow. Do you have a manuscript or book idea that you would like us to consider for publishing? Please visit advantagefamily.com.

This book is dedicated to my father, Dr. Donald L. Perryman, and my mother, Willetta M. Perryman. Among many other things, I thank my father for teaching me how to learn, and I thank my mother for teaching me how to teach.

FOREWORD

DR. BENJAMIN E. MAYS, one of the world's greatest educators and orators, once stated, "Every man and woman is born into the world to do something unique and something distinctive." Because I am a long-time education researcher, leader, practitioner, and consultant, these words resonate deeply in me. I believe with all my heart and soul that all students—regardless of race, color, national origin, religion, sex, age, and disability—have something valuable and unique they can contribute to the world. But when the rubber meets the road in the classroom environment, educators too often fail to share and operate with this view by teaching only to the most receptive, motivated, and privileged students. Another basic truth that I hold is that all students are unique, with wide-ranging and multidimensional talents, interests, and intellectual and imaginative capabilities. I also hold the viewpoint that it is critical that the multifaceted dimensions of Black children are acknowledged, affirmed, and lifted across the curriculum and through the day-to-day schooling interactions with their teachers, as well as in their homes with their families.

In *Elevating Futures: A Model for Empowering Black Elementary Student Success*, Dr. Tracee Perryman offers important insights and perspectives on inspiring Black children. She does a great job of incorporating personal experiences with some of the best scholarship and research on Black children and the positive and negative aspects of their learning. Both descriptive and introspective in nature, she also notes the importance of after-school programming in the intellectual, social, and emotional development of Black children.

This book arrives with our nation in a fragile state. In the summer of 2020, the largest civil rights demonstration in the history of the United States was sparked by the death of George Floyd—like that of so many other people of color—during a brutal encounter with police officers. As America awoke to the harsh reality that those from marginalized communities had known for generations, the examination of how we might police differently cracked open the door to a broader discussion of job opportunities, educational outcomes, and other basic inequities haunting American society.

At the same time, a ceaseless, borderless global pandemic has shattered our illusions and lifted the veil from our eyes as society begins to view the gap between the haves and have-nots reaching epic proportions. As nearly every educator in America can tell you, the poorest and least equipped students are falling farther behind as they navigate new technological hurdles and uncertain schedules. And today's political leadership seems unable or unwilling to provide answers as major segments of American society sit stuck in a quagmire of increasingly dysfunctional and partisan politics. As society seeks better answers on how to bring greater equity to American classrooms, particularly when it comes to educating vulnerable, Black children, Dr. Perryman has arrived in the nick of time with a child-centered, culturally competent, research-centered program to lift up those in need.

I have always admired that Dr. Perryman's educational approach is grounded in the trial and error that only hands-on experience can give you. By listening closely to her students in her after-school programs and following her instincts, she has developed an innate sense of how to inspire Black children. But to develop a coherent, pedagogically consistent approach, she needed to absorb and analyze scientific theories, frameworks, and models that she has been deliberately applying on the front lines. It is clear that she benefited from the intellectual footing offered through the rigor of doctoral study. The beauty of the intellectual experience at the Ohio State University—and institutions of similar breadth and depth found around the world—is in the collegial environment and cross-pollination of subjects and discipline that it takes to pursue greater understanding of different social phenomena.

With the right temperament and gritty determination, former doctoral students like Dr. Perryman become greater than the sum of their collective parts as they learn from the work of others while on the existential quest of intellectual destination. Just as all students have something to contribute, teachers and professors also have something that they can learn from their students or mentees—nuggets of wisdom to carry and eventually make as their combined or shared creations. This book is a product of that and a representation of the power of mentor-mentee relationships that lead to deeper discovery and meaning. I am honored to write a foreword for Dr. Perryman's book.

In my humble opinion, she illuminates the path that can help "elevate" all of our young people, especially Black children from fragile schools and communities in America. I am confident that this book will allow individuals to enter the complicated world of educating vulnerable, Black children and understanding the many social dilemmas in which they frequently find themselves in their schools, neighborhoods, and communities. In closing, I believe that those individuals—teachers, school counselors, after-school professionals, etc.—who come into daily contact with such Black children will find this book useful and enriching. Thank you, Dr. Perryman, for gifting the education community with this precious resource.

JAMES L. MOORE III, PHD
Vice Provost for Diversity and Inclusion and Chief
Diversity Officer, the Ohio State University

INTRODUCTION

As a society, we have wasted too many resources trying to make Black children meet our objectives. Now it's time to give them a real voice in their achievement and their success.

—DR. TRACEE PERRYMAN

MY FATHER, DR. DONALD L. PERRYMAN, received his bachelor's and master's of business administration degrees from the University of Toledo, his doctor of ministry from United Theological Seminary, and his master of arts and PhD from Antioch University Graduate School of Leadership and Change. That my father would have these higher education opportunities available to him was not left to chance. They were a result of my grandmother's determination and firm belief that her children could and should attain the same things that the privileged had at their fingertips but were not readily accessible to people of color. That same profound sense of worth not just in myself but also in the belief that all children are worthy, can learn, and can succeed was instilled in me by my parents.

My mother, Willetta Perryman, taught me to read at the age of two and was later recruited to serve as a mentor and youth leader in her community. After years of positive gains and recognition in her local community, Willetta decided to follow in her father's footsteps, a man who was an Alabama schoolteacher during Jim Crow, to pursue education professionally. In 1993 Willetta became an educator for Toledo Head Start, where she was recognized for the innovative cultural, visual, and performing arts programs and parent engagement initiatives she brought to her classroom. Willetta moved on from Head Start to open her own educational centers, receiving accolades in 2011 and a literacy award in 2018 from the Ohio Department of Education for the gains her students made as a result of her vision and direction.

It is the culmination and continuous influence and support of my parents that, as a young adult, I felt a deep responsibility to cultivate the same belief in all children of color, particularly Black children, that my parents had instilled in me and to assure that the resources my parents made available to me were available to the children who need them most. And so my journey began.

My first involvement with teaching children was through my church. I was eighteen years old, and I was teaching three- to seven-year-olds in choir. Their energy was infectious. They were bright, happy, unafraid to ask questions and to engage and share what was on their minds. I worked with this same group of children over the next couple of years. As the seven-year-olds became eight- and nine-year-olds, I found that the spark that was so infectious just a year or two ago was already beginning to fade. I couldn't help but wonder why. Same minds, same abilities, but over time they had become self-conscious and stopped engaging freely.

After I left my role with the choir to oversee the church's tutoring program, I kept tabs on my choir students and was dismayed to hear that, for many, their level of disengagement increased with each passing year. It was one thirteen-year-old student's interaction that ignited the insight that set me on my current path. This boy's grades had deteriorated over the past year. He was withdrawn and beginning to get into trouble. In one class he was asked to write an essay about something that was important to him. His teacher shared his essay with me. This student wrote the most sophisticated essay on school lunches and the lack of nutrition and how the school could improve them. This disengaged thirteen-year-old boy included policy recommendations for his school. This was an intelligent child, a child with gifts, a child capable of learning.

That experience confirmed what I believed all along. It's not the child's brain. It's not their ability to learn. It's about whether they have the opportunity to exercise their individual gifts. And oftentimes in urban schools, when they have such diversity, ability, and experience, those children don't always get the opportunity to express themselves the way they would like. I began to listen to my students well enough to find out what was important to them in the present moment and developed ways to tie what was important to them into their learning goals.

My studies began in earnest in 1997 when I started my undergraduate studies in psychology at the University of Michigan. After my graduation Willetta and I cofounded the nonprofit organization Center of Hope Family Services (CHFS). Armed with a degree in psychology, I now understood why and how children learn, but it was through my mother's mentorship that I learned how to translate that knowledge into the hands-on process of classroom teaching. It was Willetta who educated me on the importance of slowing down, observing, and assessing each child as the person they are and how they learn and adapting the curriculum accordingly as opposed to trying to force every student to learn the material that we want them to learn in the way they we want them to.

Together we created CHFS in an effort to give back to and elevate our community through the improvement of life outcomes for children, adults, and families in urban settings. Our initial services included homework help/assistance, educational enrichment, youth mentoring, and food programs. This setting provided me the opportunity to implement what I had learned in real time while researching and developing culturally competent and contextually relevant adaptations to best practices in the areas of education and family empowerment through my direct experience with the children and families participating in CHFS's programs.

After graduating with honors from the University of Michigan, I went on to earn a master's degree in mental health counseling from Bowling Green State University, where I also taught and supervised education students majoring in early childhood education. The more knowledge I gained, the more passionate my research and my goal of delivering solutions to communities of color became.

Finding My Purpose

"I want to gain the knowledge necessary to help marginalized communities advocate for the resources they need to survive and thrive."

That was my statement of purpose on my PhD program application to the Ohio State University (OSU) College of Social Work. That statement was born of years of frustration providing educational enrichment and family support programs that were highly effective but were endlessly met with excuses from funders and policy makers, excuses for why they continuously underinvested in programs built by or for communities of color, excuses for why they continuously invested in the same organizations that, year after year, profited from serving communities of color while failing to provide those communities with any meaningful benefits.

When I set foot on the OSU campus in September 2010, I was ready to do the work to address the glaring educational disparities I saw for Black children. The disparities in reading and math achievement gnawed at me and fueled my desire to research the deep-seated, systemic practices designed to withhold access to a quality education from Black people since our initial journey to the United States. I studied how structural oppression changed forms from one century to the next and one generation to another. The deeper I delved into my studies, the more my heart was drawn to the need for access to education, which was to become my social justice calling.

I declared a minor specialization in education through which I met Dr. Adrienne Dixson, a professor at OSU's College of Education who studied directly under Gloria Ladson-Billings, the mother of Culturally Relevant Pedagogy. I studied educational administration and the politics that are unavoidable whether advocating for Black or non-Black children. I then met Dr. Carla Curtis, an associate professor at OSU's College of Social Work who challenged me to refine my focus and reconcile educational advancement for Black children and social work. At that point the holistic nature of educating and developing Black children clicked.

In an Afrocentric worldview, goals/objectives (educational access and attainment) are not disaggregated from social/emotional development, growth, and quality of living. I decided that my focus would be creating environments that foster learning, growth, acceptance, social/emotional well-being, and satisfaction for Black children and youth. Furthermore I decided that out-of-schooltime programs would be the ideal space to reconcile education, social/emotional wellness, and prevention programming.

My next challenge was how to operationalize the cultural richness of the strategies, frameworks, and best practices for Black children in a way that can be adapted, translated, and replicated. It was at this time that Dr. James Moore III, vice provost for diversity and inclusion and chief diversity officer at OSU, introduced me to racial socialization theory. I was amazed at its constructs as well as its validated measures for evaluating specific conversations that Black adults have with Black children. Combining racial socialization theory, Culturally Relevant Pedagogy, and other culturally affirming strategies, I began to examine the relationships between culturally relevant interventions, such as racial socialization theory, and social emotional measures, such as violence.

Past research indicated that racial socialization theory correlated with positive outcomes among Black youth, including reduction in problem behaviors,[1] anger,[2] fighting,[3] internalizing and externalizing behavior,[4] depression symptoms,[5] substance abuse,[6] and forms

---

[1]   M. O. Caughy et al., "Profiles of Racial Socialization among African American Parents: Correlates, Context, and Outcome," *Journal of Child and Family Studies* 20 (2011): 491–502, https://doi.org/10.1007/s10826-010-9416-1.

[2]   H. C. Stevenson et al., "Racism Stress Management: Racial Socialization Beliefs and the Experience of Depression and Anger in African American Youth," Youth and Society 29, no. 2 (1997): 197–222, https://doi.org/10.1177/0044118X97029002003.

[3]   E. W. Neblett Jr. et al., "Patterns of Racial Socialization and Psychological Adjustment: Can Parental Communications about Race Reduce the Impact of Racial Discrimination?," *Journal of Research on Adolescence* 18, no. 3 (2008): 477–515.

[4]   C. A. Elmore and N. K. Gaylord-Harden, "The Influence of Supportive Parenting and Racial Socialization Messages on African American Youth Behavioral Outcomes," Journal of Child and Family Studies 22, no. 1 (2013): 63–75, https://doi.org/10.1007/s10826-012-9653-6.

[5]   L. L. Liu et al., "Teaching about Race/Ethnicity and Racism Matters: An Examination of How Perceived Ethnic Racial Socialization Processes Are Associated with Depression Symptoms," Cultural Diversity and Ethnic Minority Psychology 19 (no. 4), 383–94, https://doi.org/10.1037/a0033447; E. W. Neblett Jr. et al., "Racial Identity Mediates the Association between Ethnic-Racial Socialization and Depressive Symptoms," Cultural Diversity and Ethnic Minority Psychology 19 no. 2 (2013): 200–207, https://doi.org/10.1037/a0032205.

[6]   S. A. Wallace et al., "Gold Diggers, Video Vixens, and Jezebels: Stereotype Images and Substance Use among Urban African American Girls," *Journal of Women's Health* 20, no. 9 (2011): 1315–24.

of criminal behavior.[7] A closer look at the data revealed another interesting relationship: the study participants reported significantly more messages related to racial discrimination than racially affirming messages.[8] Alertness to racial discrimination is essential to developing coping/survival strategies; however, it is also important to balance alertness to discrimination with cultural affirmation.

These findings further fueled my desire to develop a framework that balances racial trauma exposure/preparation skills with the richness of African American culture and the numerous instances in which Black people have overcome racial terror, trauma, barriers, and oppression. The after-school programming framework I envisioned would also affirm the individual and collective identity of African Americans in the United States. I needed additional skills to develop the after-school programming I envisioned, and I was fortunate to have Dr. Tamara Davis as my dissertation chair to help fill that gap. In 2016 Dr. Davis was associate dean for Academic Affairs and Graduate Studies Committee chair in the College of Social Work at OSU. It was Dr. Davis who taught me how to translate my passion for educational equity into nonprofit management and helped me develop my skills as an advocate speaking to policy makers.

Now more than ten years from the time I began my research at OSU, not enough progress has been made. Ongoing racial disparities in academic performance continue to indicate that African American children and youth need increased attention in after-school interventions, yet despite the state department of education resolutions requesting culturally relevant interventions to promote

---

7   C. H. Burt et al., "Racial Discrimination, Ethnic-Racial Socialization, and Crime: A Microsociological Model of Risk and Resilience," American Sociological Review 77, no. 4 (2012): 648–77; C. H. Burt et al., "Interpersonal Racial Discrimination, Ethnic-Racial Socialization, and Offending: Risk and Resilience among African American Females," Justice Quarterly 32, no. 3 (2015): 532–70.

8   A. Harris-Britt et al., "Perceived Racial Discrimination and Self-Esteem in African American Youth: Racial Socialization as Protective Factor," Journal of Research on Adolescence 17, no. 4 (2007): 669–82.

African American youth achievement, few tangible interventions are prescribed nor guidance provided on which interventions may work best for Black children. With this lack of movement from our society's educational system, how do we counter the repeated instances of police brutality against Blacks in America that our children are exposed to? Educators, parents, and community members must initiate strong, informed, intentional efforts to combat the social/emotional effects of such racism with culturally affirming programs that reinforce positive individual and collective identity and inspire growth and achievement—despite the odds.

The publicly exposed killings of Blacks by law enforcement have elicited more awareness of the needs of Black children and families, including reducing racial disparities in education, justice system involvement, and mental health. However, this awareness, yet again, has not resulted in any significant positive structural changes to our education, justice, or mental health systems. This lack of progress has served to deepen my drive to answer the call to deliver solutions to communities of color, children, families, educators, social service providers, and advocates.

A plethora of research has been conducted on after-school program effectiveness and the implementation of best practices. By and large the positive results have not translated into after-school program settings. Currently $1.2 billion is allocated by the United States Department of Education annually to implement after-school programs that are intended to improve academic performance and social/emotional development and increase parental engagement.

Out of the 1.6 million students served annually, African American children account for nearly 320,000 of them (United States Department of Education, 2019). In 2018–2019 states reported that 48.2 percent of students improved English grades in elementary, and 54.9 percent of students were considered as regularly attending. (*Regular* is defined as attendance for more than thirty days during the academic year.)[9] And even less is known about whether after-school programs benefit African American children and youth, as racially disaggregated data is virtually nonexistent. We must believe and invest in children of color and, in particular, Black children.

This edition of ELEVATE! After School focuses on a K-3 curriculum that closes the achievement gaps and ensures equity of opportunities for students of color in urban communities through the implementation of an established framework with ready-to-follow strategies. The ELEVATE! program strategies integrate tools to help Black children cope with racism, discrimination, and structural oppression through the development of a positive sense of self and racial group identity, high expectations for achievement, self-efficacy to excel, and motivation to elevate and be elevated by their community.

Drawing from my educational, personal, and professional experiences working with Black children, youth, and families, I will outline ELEVATE!'s six-pronged strategy that integrates academic, social/emotional, and cultural enrichment that has achieved the following results:

During the 2019–2020 school year at Martin Luther King Jr. Elementary School, ELEVATE! students

- showed an improvement in their reading grade point average,

- showed an improvement in their math grade point average,

- demonstrated an increase in their school day attendance, and

- reduced their total number of unexcused absence hours.

---

9   Overview of the Nita M. Lowey 21st Century Learning Centers (21st CCLC) Annual Performance Data: 2018–2019 US Department of Education, Office of Elementary and Secondary Education, 21st Century Community Learning Centers, 4 and 10.

During the 2019–2020 school year at Old West End Elementary School (OWE), ELEVATE! students

- showed an improvement in their English/language arts grade point average,

- showed significant increases in school day attendance rate,

- decreased their rate of chronic absenteeism, and

- achieved an 89 percent after-school program attendance rate.

During the 2019–2020 school year at Robinson Elementary School, ELEVATE! students

- showed an improvement in their reading grade point average,

- maintained an excellent school day attendance rate, and

- reduced their total number of unexcused absence hours.

During 2018–2019 at Martin Luther King Jr. Elementary School (MLK),

- the percentage of participants who scored on or above grade level on Edmentum reading diagnostics rose from 32 percent to 60 percent;

- 84 percent of participants scored on or above grade level on Edmentum math diagnostics at the end of the year;

- 66 percent of participants were regular attendees (thirty days or more);

- 100 percent of regular attendees scored proficient or above on the Ohio Computer-Based Assessment (OCBA) in math in 2019;

- key stakeholders agreed that the program environment was conducive to positive youth development (PYD);

- 100 percent of parents reported that the ELEVATE! program helped their children at least somewhat with getting along with other students, with 91 percent reporting that it helped "very much";

- 100 percent of parents agreed that the ELEVATE! program staff cared about their children and wanted to see them succeed;

- 100 percent of staff reported that the ELEVATE! program helped students at least somewhat with social skills/interacting with others; and

- 82 percent of parents who responded to our annual survey reported that they had been to a family event hosted by the ELEVATE! program in the past year, and 80 percent agreed that the program informed them about resources and supports in the community.

During the 2018–2019 school year at OWE,
- the rate of regularly attending students (thirty days or more) who scored on or above grade level on the Edmentum reading diagnostics rose from 46 percent to 69 percent;

- 75 percent of the participants scored on or above grade level on the Edmentum math diagnostics at the end of the year;

- 97 percent of the participants were regular attendees;

- 98 percent of parents reported that the ELEVATE! program helped their children at least somewhat in getting along with other students; and

- 80 percent of students reported that the ELEVATE! program helped them at least somewhat to make choices that helped them stay out of trouble.

That this book and the ELEVATE! curriculum it outlines are urgently needed in 2021 is an indication of how we must continue to strive, as my grandmother did, to achieve not only equal access to education for all but also the belief that all children are capable of learning. Let's help our students Shine, Learn, Grow, Strive, Work, and Rise Together!

THE ELEVATE! FRAMEWORK

Forces of negativity designed to shame me out of pursuing my dreams, but faith and hope will sustain me. I'll always believe, so I will succeed. Just watch me ELEVATE! higher and higher.

—DR. TRACEE PERRYMAN

HOW CAN WE MOTIVATE students in after-school programs to attend regularly, to enjoy participating, and to develop academic and social/emotional skills, and how can we achieve these goals through an organized, engaging program that is easy for after-school program teachers to use? It is the answers to these questions on which the ELEVATE! framework and subsequent detailed curriculum was developed. The teacher is a key component to the implementation of any curriculum, and the ELEVATE! curriculum, no matter how robust and impactful, can only truly be effective if the teacher or practitioner fully believes that

➡ *all* children are capable of learning;

➡ all children, particularly Black children, can succeed academically;

➡ racial achievement gaps can be narrowed and closed if both students and after-school program facilitators are equipped with the proper tools; and

➡ Black and urban children are deserving of the same time, commitment, and resources as their non-Black and nonurban counterparts.

Do you believe, and are you ready to instill that belief in your students?

ELEVATE! Influences

Rooted in the theoretical framework of racial socialization theory, ELEVATE! honors the African roots of Black children and seeks to restore cultural identity and expand opportunity for Black children living in cities. The framework for our curriculum is built upon a rich legacy of cultural stories and solid, evidence-based academic research. A foundational study by Boykin and Toms proposed that attitudes, values, and skills transmitted through racial socialization are rooted in the West African cultural ethos.[10] These researchers identified nine cultural dimensions common to those of West African descent. These dimensions inform this after-school curriculum for fostering Black children's academic, social, and emotional resilience.

These qualities include the following:

---

10   A. Boykin and F. D. Toms, "Black Child Socialization: A Conceptual Framework," in Black Children: Social, Educational, and Parental Environments, eds. H. P. McAdoo and J. McAdoo, (Beverly Hills, CA: Sage, 1985), 33–51.

1. Spirituality—conducting one's life as though its essence were vitalistic rather than mechanistic and as though transcending forces significantly govern the lives of people.

2. Harmony—placing a premium on versatility and placing an emphasis on wholeness rather than discreteness.

3. Movement—approaching life rhythmically, particularly as expressed through the patterned interwoven mosaic of music, movement, and percussiveness.

4. Verve—psychological affinity for variability and intensity of stimulation, particularly stimulation emanating from the movement mosaic complex.

5. Affect—a premium placed on emotional sensibilities and expressiveness.

6. Communalism—sensitivity to the interdependence of people and the notion that group concerns transcend individual strivings.

7. Expressive individualism—a premium attached to the cultivation of distinctiveness, spontaneity, and uniqueness of self-expression.

8. Orality—a special emphasis on oral and aural modes of communication, especially the use of the spoken word to convey deep textural meanings not possible through the written word.

9. Social time perspective—a commitment to time as a social phenomenon much more than a concoction objectively drawn through clocks, calendars, and other inanimate markers.

In addition to the influence of racial socialization theory, the ELEVATE! curriculum has been enriched by the principles of Culturally Relevant Pedagogy and the research and practice of after-school program best practices informed by PYD theory.

CULTURALLY RELEVANT PEDAGOGY

The concept of collectivism that is embedded in the West African cultural ethos aligns with Gloria Ladson-Billings's Culturally Relevant Pedagogy, which asserts that academic success for Black students is rooted in bicultural competence (an individual's internationalization of more than one culture to function effectively and maintain healthy interpersonal relationships in those cultures) and sociopolitical consciousness (an individual's ability to critically analyze the political, social, and economic forces shaping society and one's status in it). A primary component of Ladson-Billings's pedagogy is establishing high expectations for each student's abilities, uniqueness, achievements, and role in and connections to their culture and communities.

In the classroom it is the teacher who must set the expectations that encourage students to reach their full potential. Ladson-Billings indicates that a teacher's perception of themselves and others is key to culturally relevant teaching practices. Teachers who practice culturally relevant methods see themselves as viable members of a community, believe all students can succeed, and strongly identify with teaching, whereas teachers who practice assimilation see themselves as taskmasters who provide all students the same information in the same manner and do not believe that all students are capable of succeeding. Assimilation teaching negates what culturally relevant teaching embraces—the opportunity for students to make connections between what they are learning and their individual cultural, community, and global identities.

Culturally Relevant	Assimilationist
1 Teacher sees herself as an artist, teaching, as an art.	**1** Teacher sees herself as a technician, teaching as a technical task.
2 Teacher sees herself as part of the community and teaching as giving something back to the community, encourages students to do the same.	**2** Teacher sees herself as an individual who may or may not be a part of the community; she encourages achievement as a way to escape community.
3 Teacher believes all students can succeed.	**3** Teacher believes failure is inevitable for some.
4 Teacher helps students make connections between their community, national, and global identities.	**4** Teacher homogenizes students into one "American" identity.
5 Teacher sees teaching as "pulling knowledge out"—like "mining."	**5** Teacher sees teaching as "putting knowledge into"—like "banking."

Conceptions of Self and Others

The attributes of culturally relevant teaching methods versus assimilation are further broken down to address social relations (such as *Teacher-student relationship is fluid, humanely equitable, extends to interactions beyond the classroom and into the community* versus *Teacher-student relationship is fixed, hierarchical, and limited to formal classroom roles*) and conceptions of knowledge (for example, *Knowledge is always evolving and is recycled, recreated, and shared by teacher and student alike* versus *Knowledge is static and passed from teacher to student only*). Each unit in the ELEVATE! program encompasses culturally relevant teaching methods in which to fully engage students in the lessons.

POSITIVE YOUTH DEVELOPMENT AND AFTER-SCHOOL PROGRAMS

Positive youth development is a framework rooted in the theoretical traditions of developmental psychology that emphasizes nurturing the person's many potentials rather than focusing on assumed deficits and encourages youth to have agency in their own development. It is an ongoing approach that engages youth in meaningful and decision-making roles in their community, involves all youth rather than specialized groups identified as gifted or at risk, promotes community empowerment through organizational change and collaboration, and endeavors to provide long-term commitment to youth. After-school programs provide a unique opportunity to implement positive youth development during unsupervised out-of-school time.

> After controlling for child and family factors, the study found that after-school programs with staff who showed positive regard for children, offered acceptance and encouragement, provided nurturing nonverbal cues, and facilitated reciprocal interactions with children contributed to increased reading grades for second- and third-grade participants and increased math grades for second-grade participants.[11]

---

11   K. M. Pierce et al., "Specific Features of After-School Program Quality: Associations with Children's Functioning in Middle Childhood," *American Journal of Community Psychology* 45, nos. 3–4 (June 2010): 381–93.

After-school programming is an opportunity to enrich the lives of Black children. It is my goal through the ELEVATE! curriculum to empower educators to not give up on Black kids. I know it's incredibly difficult if teachers do not have the tools necessary. I know teachers want to do more than force their students to complete another worksheet or stare at endless flash cards. This is where ELEVATE!'s clear and accessible K-3 curriculum can help by providing lesson plans that are specific and detailed, that utilize themes and culturally relevant topics and methods that engage children, and that lead to measurable outcomes.

> **After-school programming is an opportunity to enrich the lives of Black children.**

It is based on this collective research and experience that ELEVATE!'s six key tenets were developed: We Shine Together, We Learn Together, We Grow Together, We Strive Together, We Work Together, and We Rise Together.

The Curriculum

The ELEVATE! curriculum provides detailed lesson plans based on designated themes that cover seven to nine months of teaching opportunities. From a social development standpoint, the lesson plans provide teachers a road map to engage children's feelings within the curriculum, to teach children how to lift themselves and one another, and to build community and harmony while providing continual motivation through music and affirmations. The information that the teacher shares through ELEVATE!'s multifaceted lessons provides the children time and experience to connect with and understand the topic rather than focusing on disconnected memorization of material that the child does not retain.

The themes outlined in ELEVATE! are Elevating Confidence, Elevating Our Circle, Elevating Cooperation, Elevating Community, Elevating Expression, Elevating into Our Future, and Elevating Hope. It is a progressive, holistic program that begins with individual identity and affirmation of confidence in oneself. We then move beyond the individual, establishing a sense of harmony and family. From there we tackle what harmony and family looks like and how each individual participates in their community through cooperation. Now the children are ready to grasp the concept of community—how to use their skills and talents to contribute to their community and the world. Next, we embrace expression and how we can use our unique methods of expression to *elevate* into our future. And finally, we explore the concept of hope and the expectancy that things can and will be better.

ELEVATE!'s Six Tenets

Each unit/theme is brought to life through the outlined methods below.

1. WE SHINE TOGETHER

- Each lesson will begin with the "ELEVATE! Affirmation" song, whose lyrics are listed at the beginning of each lesson for ease of use.

- The plan will include daily affirmations:
"Today I feel _____

_____

_____",;

"I can make my day better by _____

_____

_____",;

"I can help make _____'s day better by

_____

_____."

- Shining Together: Each lesson will include instructions to recognize specific students for their daily academic and social accomplishments.

2. WE LEARN TOGETHER

- The curriculum will include an introduction of each new theme.

- The curriculum will be divided into specific lessons targeted to the theme.

- Each lesson will highlight real people and real issues students will encounter every day in the news, in their homes, in their communities.

- The focus will be on reading and cooperative activities.

- The curriculum will feature easy-to-read illustrated books available online featuring Black characters and questions created to measure understanding and engage students more fully with the story.

- The curriculum will introduce key concepts accompanied by questions to engage students and provide opportunities for them to apply new knowledge.

- Guidelines will be provided to support students at varying levels of reading ability.

3. WE GROW TOGETHER

- Discussion questions will connect key concepts from the book to contemporary issues students may encounter in their homes and communities.

4. WE STRIVE TOGETHER

- Lesson plans will include specific, age- and grade-level goals and objectives that align with Common Core standards.

- Lesson plans will include general vocabulary from the reading selections.

- Lesson plans will include ELEVATE! Wise Words, vocabulary connected to the reading lesson designed to build language skills.

5. WE WORK TOGETHER

- Each lesson will include art/craft projects specific to the unit allowing students to grow through individual expression and grow in their public speaking confidence through presentations.

6. WE RISE TOGETHER

- A recap of key learning points will provide opportunities for students to practice and increase skills independently.

- Each lesson will conclude with an ELEVATE! superstar chant:

- [Child's name, group name, or the entire class] is a superstar.

- [Child's achievement] makes [her/him] a superstar.

- Keep shooting for the stars.

- We love to watch you *elevate*!

Each unit features songs from the ELEVATE!
music library. You can find our catalog of songs at
https://app.sellwire.net/p/2GA.

For 50 percent off, purchasers of the book can
use this PROMO code: **ADVANTAGE50**

The ELEVATE! curriculum empowers teachers to move beyond compliance and to engage students instead through genuine, culturally relevant connection. The ELEVATE! curriculum gives children a real voice in their achievement and success. When a child has agency in their learning, they will no longer participate because they are required to; they will participate because they want to.

The full ELEVATE! curriculum offers four detailed lessons for each of the seven units. In this book I provide the first lesson for each unit. On to unit 1, "Elevating Confidence."

ELEVATING CONFIDENCE

We are all here for a purpose. We are all more than enough. We just need to believe it. When we believe, we teach our children to believe it too.

—DR. TRACEE PERRYMAN

"WHERE IS IT written that intelligence needs to be determined on the basis of tests?" This was a question posed by Harvard psychologist Howard Gardner.[12] He went on to surmise that we were able to assess intellect prior to the invention of the IQ test, and we would be able to continue to assess intellect if all the standardized IQ tests in use today were to suddenly vanish.

It is time we move beyond teaching children what we want them to know and help them identify and affirm their individual

---

12   Howard Gardner, "A Multiplicity of Intelligences: In Tribute to Professor Luigi Vignolo," (1998/2004), https://howardgardner01.files.wordpress.com/2012/06/a-multiplicity-of-intelligences1.pdf.

strengths and gifts even if they don't align with standardized tests. When children's unique strengths and gifts don't align with what the tests require them to know, it is our responsibility as educators to build those connections for them. To do so we must first aid them in developing a solid sense of self that does not require external validation to build their self-confidence.

A sense of self opens the door to behaviors that increase personal efficacy and establishes a belief in one's ability to succeed academically, socially, and emotionally. How your students feel about themselves affects their level of vulnerability when they are subjected to peer pressure and other resistance they encounter in their communities.

> The adoption of a positive sense of self for African American children and adolescents is critical if they are to flourish in a society that often devalues them through negative stereotypes, assumptions, and expectations of others. Low self-esteem, low educational achievement, and increased criminal behavior are some of the theoretical links to the impact of the negative racial identity that African Americans experience.[13]

Confidence in oneself is the foundation on which we can open every child's view of the world around them and their agency to contribute positively to that world and to personally succeed.

Drawing from Gardner's theory of multiple intelligences, I aim to inspire all educators to be open to seeing and encouraging each student's varying capacities and abilities in relation to visual-spatial,

---

13   American Psychological Association, Task Force on Resilience and Strength in Black Children and Adolescents, "Resilience in African American Children and Adolescents: A Vision for Optimal Development," (Washington, DC, 2008), https://www.apa.org/pi/families/resources/resiliencerpt.pdf.

linguistic-verbal, interpersonal, intrapersonal, logical-mathematical, musical, body-kinesthetic, naturalistic, and existentialist intelligence to aid each child in discovering what makes them shine.

Visual-Spatial: Learning visually and organizing spatially.

Linguistic-Verbal: Learning through reading, listening, speaking, and writing.

Interpersonal: Learning through collaborative and cooperative interactions.

Intrapersonal: Learning through feelings, values, and attitudes.

Logical-Mathematical: Learning through reasoning and problem-solving.

Musical: Learning through songs, patterns, rhythms, instruments, and musical expression.

Body-Kinesthetic: Learning through interactions with one's environment. People with bodily kinesthetic intelligence have an ability to use their own bodies to create products, perform skills, or solve problems through mind-body union.[14]

Naturalistic: Learning through classification, categories, and hierarchies found in the natural world with respect for each natural element's role in the environment.

Existential: Learning by connecting real-world understandings and application.

In this unit you'll provide your students with a curriculum connected to *confidence*, highlighting the importance of equipping students to define themselves, create for themselves, and speak for themselves.

---

14   M. Marenus, "Gardner's Theory of Multiple Intelligences," Simply Psychology (June 9, 2020), https://www.simplypsychology.org/multiple-intelligences.html.

SPECIAL NOTES

1. Please plan a picture day during this first unit. The pictures will be used throughout the curriculum.

2. Please provide each student with their own set of cards—one red, one yellow, and one green. These will be used for sharing opinions in some of the lessons. You may choose to have them show their thumbs up, down, or sideways in place of cards if needed.

Building Confidence One Student at a Time

MICHELLE AND HALLIYAH'S STORY

Shortly after my niece Halliyah came to live with me, she began attending Center of Hope's ELEVATE! program. I knew of the program because I am a native of Toledo, Ohio, and I had previously worked with Willetta Perryman in the Toledo Head Start program. Through my work with Mrs. Perryman, I knew how wonderfully well she worked with young children and that she would have the compassion my niece would need as she continued to adjust to the passing of her mother, my younger sister. I shared with Mrs. P. that one of the things that my niece loved to do most with her mother was cook.

Through the ELEVATE! program, especially cooking with Mrs. P., I saw Halliyah gradually come out of her shell. She became more conversational; she expressed interest in wanting to learn and do different things besides being on her tablet all day. Halliyah wanted to learn how to cook and would look for recipes to cook with me and independently. Suddenly, she was wanting to do more things by herself, prepare breakfast and lunch, and research different fruits and vegetables that she hadn't tried. Now I'm not saying that she was willing to try everything, but it was wonderful to see her interests and initiative expand in researching and learning more about the new things that she was cooking and eating with the ELEVATE! cooking program.

As an educator and social worker of thirty years, currently working for the office of Head Start's national office, assisting teachers and leaders in Head Start programs across the country, I am encouraged by ELEVATE!'s high-quality program with committed staff that understand how children grow and develop holistically. ELEVATE! addresses the academic, social, emotional, cognitive, and physical well-being of their students. Through my niece's participation in the virtual program, I have seen a strong alignment between what they do on-site and in person and what they offer virtually—high-quality teaching and experiential, hands-on learning.

LESSON 1: I AM A SUPERSTAR!

We Shine Together

Lead children in the expression of daily affirmations, allowing each child to recite individually:

"Today I feel _____
_____
_____."

"I can make my day better by _____
_____
_____."

"I can help make _____'s day better by _____
_____
_____."

Together sing the "ELEVATE! Affirmation" song. Beginning each lesson with this song allows you, the teacher, to set the cultural tone for the classroom—a tone that tells the students that everyone is welcome and that each and every child will be loved and accepted for their unique traits and abilities.

Mathematicians and artists,

Musicians and lyricists,

They are all gifts;

They are loved at ELEVATE!

Athletes and readers,

Supporters and leaders,

All kinds of believers

Are loved at ELEVATE!

Hair kinky or straight,

Long tresses or a fade,

Eyes of all shapes

Are loved at ELEVATE!

Fair skin

To every shade of melanin,

We are all kin;

You are loved at ELEVATE!

A temperament that's mild

Or with a little bit of spice,

Personas of all types

Are loved at ELEVATE!;

At ELEVATE!,

Everybody can find their place.

Never have to worry about feeling hate,

Everybody's loved at ELEVATE!

We Learn Together

The "Elevating Our Confidence" curriculum will be divided into specific lessons focused on what it means to be great, to succeed, to be unique, and to *elevate*. Write the words *great, succeed, unique,* and *confidence* on the board as you discuss each.

GREAT

- ➡ Have you heard of the word *great*?

- ➡ Where did you hear the word *great*?

- ➡ Who can put the word *great* in a sentence?

- ➡ What do you think the word *great* means?

- ➡ What does it mean to be *great*?

- ➡ What types of things are going on in your life when you feel *great*?

SUCCEED

- ➡ Have you heard of the word *succeed*?

- ➡ Where did you hear the word *succeed*?

- ➡ Who said it to you?

- ➡ Who can put *succeed* in a sentence?

- ➡ What do you think the word *succeed* means?

- ➡ What does it mean to succeed?

- ➡ Tell me about a time when you succeeded.

CONFIDENCE

➡ Have you heard of the word *confidence*?

➡ Where did you hear the word *confidence*?

➡ Who said it to you?

➡ Who can put *confidence* in a sentence?

➡ What do you think the word *confidence* means?

➡ *Confidence* means "I know who I am" and that how *you* feel about yourself is most important. *You* have the power to *believe* you are *great*, no matter what anyone else may think.

UNIQUE

➡ Have you heard of the word *unique*?

➡ How would you feel if someone told you that you are unique?

➡ What do you think the word *unique* means?

➡ What does it mean for a person to be unique?

➡ What is unique about you?

➡ Does anyone else's laugh sound just like yours?

➡ Does anyone else's handwriting look just like yours?

➡ What else is uniquely you? Your voice? Maybe you have dance moves that are all your own, or you are really good at spelling difficult words.

ELEVATE

➡ Have you heard of the word *elevate*?

➡ When you practice something new, do you get better at it? Practicing elevates your abilities.

➡ Has anyone ever made you feel elevated?

➡ Have you ever made anyone feel elevated?

➡ What does it mean to elevate, and why do you think we named this program ELEVATE!?

We named this program ELEVATE! because we believe there is *greatness* and the potential for *success* in *every* child and adult that participates. That's why we call ourselves ELEVATE! superstars. We elevate how we act and learn so that we shine brighter and brighter and we rise higher and higher.

"The children in the ELEVATE! program are learning to be better students every day. They are committed to doing their homework. They are committed to doing all of their reading and all of their learning" (Erica Krause, former ELEVATE! program coordinator).

CONFIDENCE ACTIVITY

Now we're going to do a short activity about confidence so that each of you can determine how you think about yourselves, find your areas of greatness, and think about the people who bring out the greatness in you.

Teachers, be ready, through your own observations, to offer students who struggle to identify their own strengths and unique gifts. Draw from academics as well as recess (who can run fast, jump high, dribble a ball well), social (who always offers help to another student on or off the playground), and creative arts (who can sing, dance, paint).

➡ I am great because _____
_____
_____.

➡ I admire _____
because _____
_____
_____.

➡ The great things that I expect to happen for me include
_____
_____
_____
_____.

➡ I am good at _____
_____
_____
_____.

➡ My friends are good at _____
_____
_____.

➡ When I need help, I go to _____
_____
_____.

➡ Some important people who look like me are _____
_____
_____.

➡ I like to do _____
_____
_____with my free time.

This lesson features *I Am Enough* written by Grace Byers and illustrated by Keturah A. Bobo. *I Am Enough* is a lyrical ode to loving who you are, respecting others, and being kind to one another. It is recommended for preschool through grade 3. Guidelines are provided to support students at different levels of reading ability. Discussion questions will connect key concepts from the book to contemporary issues students may encounter in their homes and communities.

Let's all look at the cover of the book *I Am Enough* by Grace Byers. What do you think this story might be about? (Allow students time to share.)

Read the story to your students, integrate student readers as appropriate, or access the following read-along option on YouTube: "Story Time for Kids with POWER ASC | *I Am Enough* | Children's Book Read Aloud."

We Grow Together

DISCUSSION QUESTIONS: I AM ENOUGH

➡ Why do you think the reader said "I am enough" so many times?

➡ In the story it says, "Like the sun, I am here to shine." What do you think that means?

➡ Do you think that we are all here to shine?

➡ How can *you* shine like the sun?

➡ In the book it said that the characters were *here* to do a lot of things. Did you see any examples in the book of things you like to do or you feel you are meant to do?

➡ Did the characters look the same in the book? Did they all like to do the same things, or were they unique?

➡ What does *I Am Enough* say about unique people? After listening to this book, do you want to be unique, or does being unique or different seem scary?

➡ What sometimes happens to children who "shine like the sun," "stand out," or are "different"?

➡ How should we treat people who are unique or different?

➡ How should we respond when other people point out things about us that are unique or different?

CLOSING REFLECTIONS

I Am Enough showed us how we are each unique—we are each our own person in how we look, laugh, love, learn, believe, and think. All these things that make you *you* are enough. It's important to celebrate your uniqueness and the uniqueness of others because we are all different, and we are all enough.

We Strive Together

Lesson plans will include ELEVATE! Wise Words. The Wise Words vocabulary will be connected to the reading lesson designed to build language skills and help students meet Common Core benchmarks. Below, the focus is broken down by grade level.

Kindergartners: The goal we are striving for is letter recognition. Encourage the students to identify all the words in the story that begin with a certain letter and talk about what the word means. This can be done for multiple letters per story. Some students may be ready to advance to matching letters with sounds and identifying syllables in multisyllable words.[15]

---

15   Common Core State Standards Initiative, "English Language Arts Standards," accessed September 3, 2021, http://www.corestandards.org/ELA-Literacy/RF/K/1/d/.

First Graders: The goal to strive for is segmenting and blending phonemes, which are *perceptually distinct units of sound in a specified language that distinguish one word from another*, in other words segmenting parts of the word out and blending them together to read one syllable words. For example, "nose"—*n, o, s,* silent *e* = nose. Some students may be ready to move on to isolating and pronouncing vowel sounds along with phonemes in spoken single-syllable words.[16]

Second Graders: The goal is phonics and word recognition, beginning with identifying vowel sounds within words. Some students may be able to decode regularly spelled two-syllable words with long vowels.[17]

Third Graders: The goal is to identify prefixes and suffixes and decode multisyllable words. Third graders should be encouraged to read accurately and with increased fluency, applying phonics skills to sound out unfamiliar words and utilizing context clues to determine the meaning of those words.[18]

WISE WORDS
General Vocabulary

➡ Great

➡ Succeed

➡ Confidence

➡ Unique

---

16   Ibid., accessed September 3, 2021, http://www.corestandards.org/ELA-Literacy/RF/1/2/b/ and http://www.corestandards.org/ELA-Literacy/RF/1/2/c/.

17   Ibid., accessed September 3, 2021, http://www.corestandards.org/ELA-Literacy/RF/2/3/b/ and http://www.corestandards.org/ELA-Literacy/RF/2/3/b/.

18   Ibid., accessed September 3, 2021, http://www.corestandards.org/ELA-Literacy/RF/3/3/a/ and http://www.corestandards.org/ELA-Literacy/RF/3/3/c/.

I Am Enough Vocabulary

Grades K–1		**Grades 2–3**
Sing	Climb	Overcome
Soar	Rise	Winner
Grow	Pour	Mountains
Stand	Dream	Champ
Love	Learn	Swell
Try	Fear	Disagree
		Worth

We Work Together

This is where we allow students to expand the lesson beyond the book and apply other types of intelligence and experiences. This lesson's art/craft project enhances the topic of *confidence* by having the students create personalized tote bags. While students work on their projects, tap into one or more of the songs from ELEVATE!'s music library (https://app.sellwire.net/p/2GA) related to this lesson: "ELEVATE!," "ELEVATE! Affirmation," "ELEVATE! Superstars."

MATERIALS

Cloth tote bag, feathers, poster board, 3"–4" letter stencils, stones, fabric glue, scissors, and other decorative craft items that can stick on to the bag/fabric.

INSTRUCTIONS

Students should trace and cut out a stencil of their first and last initials. Those should go on the front of the bag. Depending on the bag and stencil sizes, the child can put their entire first name on the front of the bag. They can then glue other decorative items—stones, feathers, stickers, etc.—onto their bags. They can also use fabric to make shapes, initials, etc. and glue onto the bag. They can use this bag to carry items to and from ELEVATE!

COLLABORATIVE GROUP ACTIVITY

Allow each child to show their tote bag and how their design represents who they are.

CONCLUSION

In today's lesson we learned about what it means to be unique. We talked about elevating our confidence by recognizing and celebrating our own skills, talents, and personalities that make us special. We learned that we are always enough and that we can succeed at whatever we try to do.

We Rise Together

This is the point where you and the students review the progress for the day or the week and reinforce the lessons and unit focus. It's time to lead them in affirming their progress!

"ELEVATE! SUPERSTARS"

➡ [Child's name, group name, or the entire class] is a superstar.

➡ [Child's achievement] makes [her/him/them] a superstar.

➡ Keep shooting for the stars.

➡ We love to watch you *elevate*!

Additional Resources

Songs from the ELEVATE! music library:
(https://app.sellwire.net/p/2GA):

"ELEVATE!"
"ELEVATE! Affirmation"
"ELEVATE! Superstars"

Special Note: In unit 2 we will be creating a family tree. Please ask the students to gather birth dates of key family members before unit 2.

UNIT 2

ELEVATING OUR CIRCLE

I am because we are.

—TRADITIONAL AFRICAN WISDOM OF UBUNTU

HISTORICALLY OUR APPROACH to school discipline has been reactive. As educators we are often conditioned to wait for a child to act out or to cause a disruption and then immediately identify that child, rather than the circumstance, as a *problem child*. The result of that course of action is either to use school discipline, which often involves exclusion, to address the issue, or to ignore the issue altogether. Both of these options affect the classroom community in a negative way—fostering isolation and shame rather than unification to elevate each child and the classroom as a whole.

The Centers for Disease Control and Prevention (CDC) have found that students' sense of connectedness to their school environment is lower in schools that employ harsh and punitive discipline as opposed to those that encourage a climate of caring and supportive interpersonal relationships and a student's opportunity to have a voice in decision-making and that those schools in which the students felt more supported and connected had significantly lower average student drug use and delinquency.[19]

We should instead be fostering a unified positive classroom and school environment from the beginning rather than waiting on a child to do something wrong and then attempting to teach the positive alternative through discipline. What I advocate and encourage through the ELEVATE! curriculum is bigger than simply maintaining a code of conduct to serve as a checklist of how a person should behave but rather to embody the greater landscape of our inherent and valuable interconnectedness—to join together. Drawing from Boykin and Toms's sixth cultural dimension common to those from West African descent,[20] *communalism*—sensitivity to the interdependence of people and the notion that group concerns transcend individual strivings—is a message of interconnectedness and unity that we, as educators, must embed in our values and how we act in the classroom, from our visuals (what we display on the walls, building cleanliness and safety, how we greet each other, pride in our appearance) to what we read and discuss.

We must lead our children in building a positive social climate for themselves, teaching them how to recognize and build empathy

---

19   Centers for Disease Control and Prevention, "School Connectedness: Strategies for Increasing Protective Factors among Youth" (Atlanta, GA: US Department of Health and Human Services, 2009).

20   Boykin and Toms, "Black Child Socialization."

in their peers, how to make their peers feel affirmed when they're down, and how to be proactive. As an educator you have the opportunity to model and discuss how to do that with your students. Ask your students, "If you see a student sitting alone in the cafeteria, what can you do about it? If you see that your friend is frustrated, what can you do about it? How can you make somebody else's day better?" It is important to build that awareness early and affirm them for managing themselves, managing their classrooms, and being an integral part of creating a positive environment. In doing so they will see that everything doesn't have to come from the top down, that individually and collectively they can contribute to their circle.

Additionally this sense of group affiliation allows children who are struggling and unable to hit certain benchmarks individually to experience a sense of accomplishment as a part of a group. The group sense of accomplishment promotes student buy-in to academics because they know that they can make a contribution as a member of a team. A student who is not motivated to try to do their best on a test because they know they won't be able to score high may be motivated to do their best if they know it will improve their group's overall score.

A Unifying Message

There are so many ways to unite our children, and music is one of my favorite unifying mediums. The students at the CHFS strongly identified with the lyrics of my song "Children of Royalty," so much so that they wanted to participate in spreading its message. They also performed the song, as you can see in a video on CHFS's YouTube channel, to three hundred guests at CHFS's Christmas show. Music and dance are activities that connect students not only to one another but also to their families and the community at large.

"Children of Royalty"

When people ask how you smile through your tears,

When they ask how you stand up to your fears,

Tell them, "It's in our heritage.

We are children of—ROYALTY."

When they ask how you keep your peace of mind,

When they ask how you walk with your head high,

Tell them, "Embrace your heritage.

We are children of—ROYALTY."

When people ask how you smile through your tears,

When they ask how you stand up to your fears,

Tell them, "It's in our heritage.

We are children of—ROYALTY."

We're gonna walk—LIKE ROYALTY.

And then talk—LIKE ROYALTY.

No more hating, we're elevating—LIKE ROYALTY.

We're making moves—LIKE ROYALTY.

Dealing in truth—LIKE ROYALTY.

No more hating, we're elevating—LIKE ROYALTY.

In this unit you'll provide your students with a curriculum of interconnectedness, harmony, and family, highlighting the importance of providing students the skills to develop their empathy for others and sense of responsibility for the greater good.

LESSON 2: HARMONY IN OUR CIRCLE

We Shine Together

Lead children in the expression of daily affirmations, allowing each child to recite individually:

"Today I feel _____

_____

_____."

"I can make my day better by _____

_____

_____."

"I can help make _____'s day
better by _____

_____

_____."

Together sing the "ELEVATE! Affirmation" song. Beginning each lesson with this song allows you, the teacher, to set the cultural tone for the classroom—a tone that tells the students that everyone is welcome and that each and every child will be loved and accepted for their unique traits and abilities.

Mathematicians and artists,

Musicians and lyricists,

They are all gifts;

They are loved at ELEVATE!

Athletes and readers,

Supporters and leaders,

All kinds of believers

Are loved at ELEVATE!

Hair kinky or straight,

Long tresses or a fade,

Eyes of all shapes

Are loved at ELEVATE!

Fair skin

To every shade of melanin,

We are all kin;

You are loved at ELEVATE!

A temperament that's mild

Or with a little bit of spice,

Personas of all types

Are loved at ELEVATE!;

At ELEVATE!,

Everybody can find their place.

Never have to worry about feeling hate,

Everybody's loved at ELEVATE!

We Learn Together

The "Elevating Our Circle" curriculum addresses the concepts of *harmony* and *family*, focusing on the meaning of family and what it means to be part of it. Write the words *harmony* and *family* on the board as you discuss each.

HARMONY

➡ Have you heard of the word *harmony*?

➡ Where have you heard the word *harmony*?

➡ Who can put the word *harmony* in a sentence?

➡ What do you think *harmony* means?

➡ What does it mean to have harmony?

➡ When have you felt harmony?

FAMILY

➡ Have you ever heard of the word *family*?

➡ Where have you heard the word *family*?

➡ Who can put the word *family* in a sentence?

➡ What does *family* mean to you?

➡ Who is in your family?

➡ Is family only the people you live with?

➡ Do you feel harmony with your family?

FAMILY ACTIVITY

Now we're going to do a short activity about *family* and what it means to each one of us.

- For grades K–1, I recommend using a chalk or smart board to list each letter of the word *family* on a separate line, then ask the class to share a word or sentence that represents what family is to them. Write their suggestions next to the appropriate letter.

- For grades 2 and 3, provide each child a sheet of paper and ask them to put each letter of the word *family* on a separate line, then ask the students to write a word or sentence that represents what family means to them for each letter.

- Modification: This activity can be done as a larger group. The teacher can preprint pictures of words that represent family based on the letters making up the word *family*. Students can use their red, yellow, and green cards to choose as a group which pictures they would like reflected, or they can use thumbs up, thumbs down, and thumbs in the middle to vote.

Thank you everyone for contributing. You just created what are called acrostic poems. Has anyone done acrostic poems before? Acrostic poems are created by using the first letter of each word to make the lines.

Now everyone can share their acrostic poems. As we listen to these poems, let's think about the following:

- What makes up a family?

- Do they have to be blood relatives? Do they have to live in our house?

- Is ELEVATE! a family? Why or why not?

- How do we treat our fellow family members?

- How *should* we treat our fellow family members?

- How should we treat our family members in ELEVATE!?

- Does family represent harmony?

- Do you think harmony is important? Why or why not?

- What other groups of people, besides family, come together in harmony (teams, classrooms, church, work)?

This lesson features *Stevie*, written and illustrated by John Steptoe. *Stevie* is a timeless classic about what it means to be family and was written by John when he was just sixteen years old. It was John's hope that his books would lead children, especially African American children, to feel pride in their origins and in who they are. "I am not an exception to the rule among my race of people," he said, accepting the Boston Globe–Horn Book Award for Illustration, "I am the rule. By that I mean there are a great many others like me where I come from."

It is recommended for grades K–3. Guidelines are provided to support students at different levels of reading ability. Discussion questions will connect key concepts from the book to contemporary issues students may encounter in their homes and communities.

Look at the cover of the book *Stevie*.

- What do you think this story might be about?

- What do you think about the two boys on the cover? Do you think they are family?

- Where does it look like they might be?

- Do you think they can teach us something about how to treat our family and our ELEVATE! family?

Read the story to your students, integrate student readers as appropriate, or access the following read-along option on YouTube: "Sesame Street—Gordon reads *Stevie* by John Steptoe—1969."

We Grow Together

DISCUSSION QUESTIONS: STEVIE

➡ Were Robert and Stevie blood brothers?

➡ Why did Robert's mother look after Stevie?

➡ What did Robert think of Stevie (that he was a pest)?

➡ What were some of the things Stevie did that bothered Robert (crawled on his bed, played with his toys, was a crybaby)?

➡ Why do you think Robert's mother let Stevie crawl on the bed, play with his toys, and cry?

➡ How did Robert, his mother, and Stevie function like a family?

➡ How do we treat our little brothers and sisters or other children who may need extra support? How *should* we treat them?

➡ How do we handle situations when our siblings or our ELEVATE family members get on our nerves? How *should* we handle those situations?

➡ How did Robert feel when Stevie moved away? Did he realize that he might have taken Stevie for granted?

CLOSING REFLECTIONS

After reading *Stevie* we saw an example of people who were not blood relatives, but they functioned like a family. We read about how being in our families is not always easy and fun, but we have to remember to stay grateful for the time that we have with the special people in our lives.

We Strive Together

Lesson plans will include ELEVATE Wise Words. The Wise Words vocabulary will be connected to the reading lesson designed to build language skills and help students meet Common Core benchmarks. Below, the focus is broken down by grade level.

"The ELEVATE program sets high expectations, and my kids know that" (Tiera Parker, mother of an ELEVATE student).

Kindergartners: The goal we are striving for is letter recognition. Encourage students to identify all the words in the story that start with a certain letter and then talk about what that word means. This can be done for multiple letters per story. Some students may be ready to advance to matching letters with sounds and identifying syllables in multisyllable words.[21]

First Graders: The goal to strive for is segmenting and blending phonemes, *perceptually distinct units of sound in a specified language that distinguish one word from another*, in other words segmenting parts of the word out and blending them together to read one syllable words. For example, "nose"—*n*, *o*, *s*, silent *e* = nose. Some students

> **"The ELEVATE! program sets high expectations, and my kids know that" (Tiera Parker, mother of an ELEVATE! student).**

---

21   Common Core State Standards Initiative, "English Language Arts Standards," accessed September 3, 2021, http://www.corestandards.org/ELA-Literacy/RF/K/1/d/.

may be ready to move on to isolating and pronouncing vowel sounds along with phonemes in spoken single-syllable words.[22]

Second Graders: The goal is phonics and word recognition, beginning with identifying vowel sounds within words. Some students may be able to decode regularly spelled two-syllable words with long vowels.[23]

Third Graders: The goal is to identify prefixes and suffixes and decode multisyllable words. Third graders should be encouraged to read accurately and with increased fluency, applying phonics skills to sound out unfamiliar words and utilizing context clues to determine the meaning of those words.[24]

WISE WORDS

General Vocabulary

➡ Family

➡ Harmony

➡ Acrostic

Stevie Vocabulary

Grades K–1	**Grades 2–3**
Look	Friends
Bed	Spoiled
Toys	Company

cont'd on next page

---

22 Ibid., accessed September 3, 2021, http://www.corestandards.org/ELA-Literacy/RF/1/2/b/ and http://www.corestandards.org/ELA-Literacy/RF/1/2/c/.

23 Ibid., accessed September 3, 2021, http://www.corestandards.org/ELA-Literacy/RF/2/3/b/ and http://www.corestandards.org/ELA-Literacy/RF/2/3/b/.

24 Ibid., accessed September 3, 2021, http://www.corestandards.org/ELA-Literacy/RF/3/3/a/ and http://www.corestandards.org/ELA-Literacy/RF/3/3/c/.

Grades K–1	Grades 2–3
Old	Greedy
Loud	Breadbox
Live	Nerves
Fun	Boogeyman
	Marshmallows

We Work Together

This is where we allow students to expand the lesson beyond the book and apply other types of intelligence and experiences. This lesson's art/craft project enhances the topic of *family* by creating a family tree. While students work on their projects, tap into one or more of the songs from ELEVATE!'s music library related to this lesson: "ELEVATE!," "ELEVATE! Affirmation," "ELEVATE! Superstars," "Children of Royalty."

MATERIALS

Pillowcase, fabric paint or permanent marker, stones in the color of each birth stone, glue.

INSTRUCTIONS

Each child should use their fabric paint or permanent marker to draw a tree that fills the majority of the pillowcase. Each child should create enough branches to resemble each of the family members they want to display on their family tree. They should look up the birthstone for each family member that they want to represent and glue that stone on a branch. When complete, they should paint on or write in their family name. Other craft items can be used (feathers, beads, sticky letters) to decorate.

COLLABORATIVE GROUP ACTIVITY

Allow each child to show their pillowcase and share the names on their family tree and what makes them special to them.

CONCLUSION

In today's lesson we talked about family and who can be a part of ours. We also talked about different types of families. They don't have to all be blood relatives. We also talked about how to treat members of our family. Use this pillowcase at home to remind you of the people who are important to you and how to treat them with special care. We want to be thankful for the time we get to spend with them and the memories we create so that, unlike Robert, we don't wait until they're gone to realize how much we love them.

We Rise Together

This is the point where you and the students review the progress for the day or the week and reinforce the lessons and unit focus. It's time to lead them in affirming their progress!

"ELEVATE! SUPERSTARS"

- ➡ [Child's name, group name, or the entire class] is a superstar.
- ➡ [Child's achievement] makes [her/him/them] a superstar.
- ➡ Keep shooting for the stars.
- ➡ We love to watch you *elevate*!

Additional Resources

Songs from the ELEVATE! music library (https://app.sellwire.net/p/2GA):

"Children of Royalty"

"ELEVATE! Affirmation"

"ELEVATE! Superstars"

Little Novel-Ties Stevie study guide

UNIT 3

ELEVATING COOPERATION

We are a village, and everyone has a part in this village.

—DR. TRACEE PERRYMAN

BY CULTIVATING CONFIDENCE and harmony among your students, you have established the foundation on which to build cooperation. When your students feel good about themselves and united as a team, do you see greater cooperation among them?

The goal of cooperation is to give children responsibility and agency in their participation in the program and in their academic outcomes. This cannot be achieved through assimilation teaching practices in which knowledge and information is fixed and is shared only from teacher to student with no opportunity or encouragement for students to provide input or ask questions. An environment that encourages curiosity and sharing of ideas will build a child's confidence and respect for others' perspectives, naturally paving the way for a willingness to cooperate.

Collective cooperation can best be fostered when the classroom is thought of as a village in which every member has a part in keeping the village running and providing for all. I continuously share this message with my students, providing examples of how they can practice cooperation in their everyday lives.

If we are in harmony, we should be able to

… play with the LEGOs without fighting, right?

… play dodgeball without hitting people in the head too hard, right?

… clean up our space at the end of the day, right?

… take care of our things and put them away properly, right?

That's all part of being a village, right?

Equally important is how educators address scenarios in which a student does not perform their responsibilities. Normally when we discipline children for not doing their part, we frame it in our disapproval, which tears down a child's personal agency and self-worth. Instead of telling a child that they didn't measure up to our expectations, tell them that they are so important to the group that when they don't do their part, they hurt the group, reinforcing that everyone has the power to choose to pull down or *elevate* the group.

Building Cooperation through Efficacy and Mattering

It is the collective responsibility of students, parents, and teachers alike to make sure every child feels special, important, loved, and appreciated. This can be accomplished by guiding children in the process of establishing a strong sense of self-efficacy and a belief that they are a person who matters in their community circles.

"Efficacy has been defined as a person's belief in their own ability to achieve certain goals and enact certain behaviors."[25]

Family is at the center of a child's initial experience with self-efficacy, and as they begin to move beyond the bounds of family and enter school, their peers begin to play a significant role in the development of their efficacy. Peers who engage with competence and confidence serve as models of confidence, and as students observe the varying abilities of their same-age peers, they begin to verify their own sense of efficacy.

"Mattering has been defined as a person's belief that they are significant, valuable, and meaningful within their environment and social settings."[26]

As with efficacy, mattering also first develops within the family unit. A child with three older siblings may struggle more with developing a sense of mattering than their oldest sibling who is able to easily demonstrate their role as helper to their younger siblings. How a child's initial sense of mattering is developed in their family circle will affect the level of guidance and experience they will need to build their sense of mattering when they enter the school environment.

---

25   R. F. Catalano et al., "Positive Youth Development in the United States: Research Findings on Evaluations of Positive Youth Development Programs," Annals of the American Academy of Political and Social Science 591, no. 1 (2004): 98–124.

26   A. L. Dixon et al., "The Adolescent Mattering Experience: Gender Variations in Perceived Mattering, Anxiety, and Depression," Journal of Counseling and Development 87, no. 3 (2009): 302–10.

Guiding a child in developing their self-efficacy (the focus of unit 1, "Elevating Confidence") and sense of mattering (the focus of unit 2, "Elevating Our Circle") serves as building blocks to guiding a child toward a sense of cooperation. A child with a strong sense of self and confidence in their abilities combined with the belief that they are important members of their family and school will be more easily encouraged, if not eager, to help others in their circle, and the more students are of service to others, the stronger their self-efficacy and sense of mattering becomes.[27]

Cooperation at Its Best

There are times in the CHFS's after-school program that the students make request for things outside the scope of our budget. In this particular case, it was the desire to have toys, for which they needed $600. They promised all the wonderful things they would and could do if they just had these toys. I let them know that funding was not unlimited and that if those items were that important to them, we could hold a fundraiser.

We decided to host a spaghetti dinner they could invite their families to. The children were 100 percent involved in coordinating the event. We broke them into four teams: (1) budget and shopping, (2) invitations, (3) table setting and decorations, and (4) greeters and entertainment. ELEVATE!'s staff cooked the dinner, and some of the parents jumped in to help serve the meal.

---

27   M. A. Zimmerman et al., "Youth Empowerment Solutions: Evaluation of an After-School Program to Engage Middle School Students in Community Change," Health Education and Behavior 45, no. 1 (2017). Retrieved from https://www.ncbi.nlm.nih.gov/pmc/articles/PMC5816934/.

The spaghetti dinner that the students organized and hosted met their goal of $600. In the end they were so proud of themselves for working together to make this a success that they no longer cared about the toys they were raising the money to buy.

In this unit, you'll provide your students with a curriculum connected to cooperation and gratitude, highlighting the importance of an individual's power to *elevate* their community through cooperation and gratitude.

LESSON 3: ATTITUDE OF GRATITUDE

We Shine Together

Lead children in the expression of daily affirmations, allowing each child to recite individually:

"Today I feel _____
_____
_____."

"I can make my day better by _____
_____
_____."

"I can help make _____'s day
better by _____
_____
_____."

Together sing the "ELEVATE! Affirmation" song. Beginning each lesson with this song allows you, the teacher, to set the cultural tone for the classroom—a tone that tells the students that everyone is welcome and that each and every child will be loved and accepted for their unique traits and abilities.

Mathematicians and artists,

Musicians and lyricists,

They are all gifts;

They are loved at ELEVATE!

Athletes and readers,

Supporters and leaders,

All kinds of believers

Are loved at ELEVATE!

Hair kinky or straight,

Long tresses or a fade,

Eyes of all shapes

Are loved at ELEVATE!

Fair skin

To every shade of melanin,

We are all kin;

You are loved at ELEVATE!

A temperament that's mild

Or with a little bit of spice,

Personas of all types

Are loved at ELEVATE!;

At ELEVATE!,

Everybody can find their place.

Never have to worry about feeling hate,

Everybody's loved at ELEVATE!

We Learn Together

The "Elevating Our Cooperation" curriculum will be divided into specific lessons focused on how cooperation builds us up individually and as a community and on gratitude for those in our community. Write the words *cooperation*, *sharing*, and *gratitude* on the board as you discuss each.

COOPERATION

- ➡ Have you ever heard of the word *cooperation*?

- ➡ Where have you heard the word *cooperation*?

- ➡ Who can put the word *cooperation* in a sentence?

- ➡ What do you think *cooperation* means?

- ➡ Imagine riding on a rocket ship. How many of you would want to go fast? Why? How many of you would want to go far? Why?

- ➡ What do you think this saying means: "If you want to fast, go alone; but if you want to go far, go in a group"?

- ➡ Think about cooperation like this: On a basketball or football team, what might happen if you're the only one playing? What might happen if you are the only one always holding and shooting the ball? Will you be able to fend off the other team, or will you need help from your teammates?

SHARING

- ➡ Have you heard of the word *sharing*?

- ➡ Where have you heard the word *sharing*?

- ➡ Who can put the word *sharing* in a sentence?

➡ What do you think *sharing* means?

➡ Is sharing sometimes a difficult thing to do?

➡ Who do you like to share with?

GRATITUDE

➡ Have you heard of the word *gratitude*?

➡ Where have you heard the word *gratitude*?

➡ Who can put the word *gratitude* in a sentence?

➡ What do you think *gratitude* means?

➡ What does it mean to have gratitude?

➡ When have you felt gratitude?

COOPERATION ACTIVITY

Now we're going to do a short activity about the themes of gratitude, sharing, and cooperation and how practicing them can help us in many ways.

You can choose to show images of the following body parts or purchase replicas: heart, lungs, brain, stomach, and skull. For feet, eyes, legs, fingers, and nose, have the students identify those parts on their own body. Ask students what the function of each of those body parts is. Then ask,

• What would happen if we didn't have each of these body parts?

• How could our feet suffer if we didn't have eyes?

• How could our heart suffer if we didn't have legs?

• How could our stomach suffer if we didn't have fingers?

- How could our stomach suffer if we didn't have a nose?

- How could our brain suffer if we didn't have a skull?

- How could our heart/legs suffer if we didn't have a brain?

So we can see that it takes cooperation from every part of our body for our bodies to work properly, and it takes cooperation for us to win on teams. It is easier for us to cooperate together as a team when we appreciate and have gratitude for all the people on our team.

This lesson features *Teamwork Isn't My Thing, and I Don't Like to Share!* written by Julia Cook and illustrated by Kelsey De Weerd. This book in the Best Me I Can Be! series teaches children that sharing and working as a team can help them get along better with others and accomplish more. It is recommended for grades K–6. Guidelines are provided to support students at different levels of reading ability. Discussion questions will connect key concepts from the book to contemporary issues students may encounter in their homes and communities.

Look at the cover of the book *Teamwork Isn't My Thing, and I Don't Like to Share!*

- What do you think this story might be about?

- Nobody looks happy on the cover. Why do you think that might be?

Read the story to your students, integrate student readers as appropriate, or access the read-along option on Kelli Franchi's YouTube channel.

We Grow Together

DISCUSSION QUESTIONS: TEAMWORK ISN'T MY THING, AND I DON'T LIKE TO SHARE!

➡ Why do you think that the main character's definition of *team* was "Together Everybody Acts Mean"?

➡ Why was the main character's (RJ's) team unsuccessful? How come they couldn't *elevate*? Did they appreciate everyone's talents?

➡ What are some ideas for how to work with someone you think is acting mean?

➡ What are some things you can offer to a team (strengths)?

➡ Why can we get more done when we work together? It's like the quote we talked about earlier: "When you go with a team, you can go further."

➡ How did RJ's coach explain the importance of cooperation, sharing, and gratitude?

CLOSING REFLECTIONS

RJ learned that when he cooperated with his teammates *and* his classmates, everyone was able to get more done, didn't have to work so hard, and had more fun. No one has every strength nor every resource, so we get farther when we ask for help and are willing to help others. RJ also learned that when he shared, he was happier and got along better with his family and his classmates, and people began to share more with him.

We Strive Together

Lesson plans will include ELEVATE! Wise Words. The Wise Words vocabulary will be connected to the reading lesson designed to build language skills and help students meet Common Core benchmarks. Below, the focus is broken down by grade level.

"My daughter loves coming to Center of Hope's after-school program. I would be lost without the ELEVATE! program because I know my daughter is in a safe place, and she is learning all the time!" (Elizabeth Cutcher, parent of an ELEVATE! student).

Kindergartners: The goal we are striving for is recognition of common high-frequency words by sight (e.g., *the, of, to, you, she, my, is, are, do, does*). Encourage students to identify these words and read them aloud.[28]

"My daughter loves coming to Center of Hope's after-school program. I would be lost without the ELEVATE! program because I know my daughter is in a safe place, and she is learning all the time!" (Elizabeth Cutcher, parent of an ELEVATE! student).

First Graders: The goal to strive for is using knowledge that every syllable must have a vowel sound to determine the number of syllables in a printed word and decoding two-syllable words following basic patterns by breaking the words into syllables.[29]

Second Graders: The goal is to master spelling-sound correspondences for additional common vowel teams and decode regularly spelled two-syllable words with long vowels.[30]

---

28   Common Core State Standards Initiative, "English Language Arts Standards," accessed September 3, 2021, http://www.corestandards.org/ELA-Literacy/RF/K/3/c/.

29   Ibid., accessed September 3, 2021, http://www.corestandards.org/ELA-Literacy/RF/1/3/d/ and http://www.corestandards.org/ELA-Literacy/RF/1/3/e/.

30   Ibid., accessed September 3, 2021, http://www.corestandards.org/ELA-Literacy/RF/2/3/b/ and http://www.corestandards.org/ELA-Literacy/RF/2/3/c/.

Third Graders: The goal is to utilize context to confirm or self-correct word recognition and understanding, rereading as necessary.[31]

WISE WORDS

General Vocabulary

- ➡ Gratitude

- ➡ Cooperation

- ➡ Work

- ➡ Together

- ➡ Appreciate

- ➡ Sharing

Teamwork Isn't My Thing, and I Don't Like to Share! Vocabulary

Grades K–1	Grades 2–3
Team	Everybody
Mean	Together
More	Achieve
New	Project
Easy	Bossy
Kid	Mummy
School	Patience
	Research
	Information
	Responsibility

---

31   Ibid., accessed September 3, 2021, http://www.corestandards.org/ELA-Literacy/RF/3/4/c/.

We Work Together

This is where we allow students to expand the lesson beyond the book and apply other types of intelligence and experiences. This lesson's gross motor, literacy, and team-building activity—Hound and Hunter, adapted from the Ultimate Camp Resource website—calls on the students to utilize cooperation in this treasure hunt game.

While students work on their projects, tap into one or more of the songs from ELEVATE!'s music library (https://app.sellwire. net/p/2GA) related to this lesson: "ELEVATE!," "ELEVATE! Affirmation," "ELEVATE! Superstars," "Children of Royalty," "When I Win, We Win."

MATERIALS

Index cards with ELEVATE! Wise Words for today. It is possible to also include Wise Words from other weeks. Hide the cards in discreet areas in a large room or outside.

INSTRUCTIONS

Split the students into teams of two. One student is the hunter, and one is the hound. The hunters stand together while their partner hounds begin to search for the cards. The hounds cannot touch the cards; instead, when they find them, they must howl until their hunter finds the card and picks it up. Neither the hunter nor hound can talk. The hunter must depend only on the hound's howl to locate the card.

COLLABORATIVE GROUP ACTIVITY

The game is over when all the cards are found or when the teacher determines sufficient time has been spent. Each group should present their cards. Teachers can give incentives based on the number of cards found, the number of cards read (or letters/syllables identified), or the number of words on each card defined.

CONCLUSION

In today's lesson, we talked about cooperation. How did you have to cooperate with your partner in the game? Was it easier to find cards when you communicated positively? Did being frustrated help the hunter find the cards any better? Cooperation and appreciation matters. Sometimes it's easier to share or cooperate in a game, but as RJ's coach said, we have to learn how to take our teamwork into the classroom.

We Rise Together

This is the point where you and the students review the progress for the day or the week and reinforce the lessons and unit focus. It's time to lead them in affirming their progress!

"ELEVATE! SUPERSTARS"

➡ [Child's name, group name, or the entire class] is a superstar.

➡ [Child's achievement] makes [her/him/them] a superstar.

➡ Keep shooting for the stars.

➡ We love to watch you *elevate*!

Additional Resources

Songs from the ELEVATE! music library
(https://app.sellwire.net/p/2GA):

"ELEVATE!"

"ELEVATE! Affirmation"

ELEVATING COMMUNITY

What is the purpose of a nation if not to empower human beings to live better together than they could individually?

—JOHN LEWIS

IVORY A. TOLDSON—professor of counseling psychology at Howard University, editor in chief of the *Journal of Negro Education*, president and chief executive of the QEM Network, and author of *No BS (Bad Stats): Black People Need People Who Believe in Black People Enough Not to Believe Every Bad Thing They Hear about Black People*—shared a training scenario for the staff of a public high school:

> I asked the participants to describe the neighborhoods of their students. I heard phrases such as "crime-ridden," "broken homes," and "drug-infested." I then asked if anyone grew up in neighborhoods that had similar characteristics. After several raised their hands, I asked, "How did

you grow up in such a neighborhood and still become successful?" This question spurred a more meaningful discussion about the neighborhoods where students are from. It was a discussion that considered *community* assets—such as hope and resilience—against a more thoughtful examination of *community* challenges.[32]

Terms like *crime-ridden*, *historically disadvantaged*, and *at-risk youth* have psychological impact on those that they describe, just as do terms like *community assets*, *hope*, and *resilience*. The first set of terms diminishes the individual and encourages those being labeled to relinquish their unique ethnic culture and community and embrace the one prescribed and defined for them.[33]

Toldson goes on to suggest that we must identify what in the community is a risk to the child rather than identifying the child as at risk, and we must build on the assets of the community to alleviate those risks. From this perspective we can build on the foundation of the hope and resilience that Toldson's participants spoke of by encouraging Black students to embrace their African culture and teaching them how they can choose to actively support those in their own communities.

Madam C. J. Walker Understood Community

I remember the first time that I introduced the concept of investing in one's community to our ELEVATE! scholars. We were discuss-

---

32   Valerie Strauss, "Why We Should Stop Labeling Students as 'At Risk'—and the Best Alternative," *Washington Post*, January 23, 2019, https://www.washingtonpost.com/education/2019/01/23/why-we-should-stop-labeling-students-risk-best-alternative/.

33   Beth Blue Swadener et al., *Children and Families "At Promise": Deconstructing the Discourse of Risk* (Albany: State University of New York Press, 1995), 1–11.

ing appreciating all different hair types. Many of our students talked about their hair being unmanageable and the struggles they had with their hair. I asked them where they purchased their hair products. In most cases I found that they did not purchase from vendors who shared or understood their heritage. I took it as an opportunity to show them the African-American-owned hair products in their neighborhoods and then went on to share with them the story of Madam C. J. Walker, who built an empire on hair care products and continuously invested in her community. It was also an opportunity to demonstrate to our children how they can build wealth by developing solutions to the problems that they face.

In this unit you'll provide your students with a curriculum connected to *giving back* and how they can help *elevate* their own *communities*. We will use a contemporary person whom they will recognize, LeBron James.

LESSON 4: WHEN I RISE, WE RISE!

We Shine Together

Lead children in the expression of daily affirmations, allowing each child to recite individually:

"Today I feel _____
_____
_____."

"I can make my day better by _____
_____
_____."

"I can help make _____'s day
better by _____
_____
_____."

Together sing the "ELEVATE! Affirmation" song. Beginning each lesson with this song allows you, the teacher, to set the cultural tone for the classroom—a tone that tells the students that everyone is welcome and that each and every child will be loved and accepted for their unique traits and abilities.

Mathematicians and artists,

Musicians and lyricists,

They are all gifts;

They are loved at ELEVATE!

Athletes and readers,

Supporters and leaders,

All kinds of believers

Are loved at ELEVATE!

Hair kinky or straight,

Long tresses or a fade,

Eyes of all shapes

Are loved at ELEVATE!

Fair skin

To every shade of melanin,

We are all kin;

You are loved at ELEVATE!

A temperament that's mild

Or with a little bit of spice,

Personas of all types

Are loved at ELEVATE!;

At ELEVATE!,

Everybody can find their place.

Never have to worry about feeling hate,

Everybody's loved at ELEVATE!

We Learn Together

The "Elevating Our Community" curriculum will be divided into specific lessons focused on the importance of each individual's contribution to their community. Write the words *community*, *giving back*, and *wealth* on the board as you discuss each.

In our time together, we've talked about the importance of elevating our confidence and how we are connected to everyone in our circle. We practice cooperation at home and at ELEVATE! by using our own unique skills and talents and respecting and appreciating those of others. We have begun to understand what being part of a *community* truly means.

Well, the reality is that every child, every adult, every family doesn't have an ELEVATE! community like you do to help them build confidence. Not everyone has the security of a loving family of students and teachers that provides them a way to contribute and be affirmed for it.

Now we're going to talk about the importance of being part of a greater whole and how, by elevating ourselves to be the best we can be, we can also elevate our communities.

COMMUNITY

➡ Have you ever heard of the word *community*?

➡ Where have you heard the word *community*?

➡ What do you think *community* means?

➡ Who can put the word *community* in a sentence?

GIVING BACK

➡ Have you ever heard of the words *giving back*?

➡ Where have you heard the words *giving back*?

➡ What do you think *giving back* means?

➡ Who can put the words *giving back* in a sentence?

WEALTH

➡ Have you heard of the word *wealth*?

➡ Where have you heard the word *wealth*?

➡ What do you think *wealth* means?

➡ Who can put the word *wealth* in a sentence?

COMMUNITY ACTIVITY

Now we're going to do a short activity about the themes of community and giving back and how supporting one another helps strengthen our communities.

Note: Teachers, you will need to provide the students real or fake dollar bills for this activity. I suggest five $1 bills per student.

Let's do an activity to show how *giving back* and *elevating* ourselves and others betters our *community*. I am going to give each of you five $1 bills. (For older groups, you can use larger units of dollars.) We have three businesses here that sell hot sneakers. Each business is represented by a basket. I need one person to hold each of these baskets. Let's come up with a name for each shoe business and put the name on the index card that's taped to the front of each basket. (For the purpose of keeping each business straight, I'll refer to them as Business A, Business B, and Business C.) I'm going to describe each business, and you will come up and put $1 (just one) in the basket of the business you want to buy shoes from based on the description I give.

- Business A gives money to programs like ELEVATE! so that we can buy supplies and treats for our ELEVATE! superstars.

- Business B gives school supplies and playground equipment to programs like ELEVATE! so that we have supplies and equipment for our superstars to use.

- Business C doesn't do any of this, but they do have cute shoes.

Put a dollar in the basket of the business that you would want to buy from based on what I just told you about each of them.

- Business A hires people who look like you and me to sell shoes in their stores, and they pay them a lot of money.

- Business B hires people who look like you and me to work in their stores, but they don't pay them very much.

- Business C doesn't do any of these things, but they do have cool commercials.

Put a dollar on the basket of the business that you would want to buy from based on what I just told you about each of them.

- Business A has shoe stores in my neighborhood.

- Business B only has shoe stores at the mall.

- Business C only sells their shoes on the internet.

Put a dollar on the basket of the business that you would want to buy from based on what I just told you about each of them.

- Business A donates money to causes that help people who look like me. They donate to causes like ending gun violence or providing more playgrounds and better schools in my neighborhood.

- Business B does not donate money to causes that help people who look like me, but they say they support causes like ending gun violence and providing better schools in my neighborhood.

- Business C doesn't donate money or support causes that help people who look like me.

Put a dollar in the basket of the business that you would want to buy from based on what I just told you about each of them.

- Business A comes out to programs like ELEVATE! and helps children learn how to read and shows children how to get high-paying jobs in the sneaker business.

- Business B donates books to programs like ELEVATE!

- Business C doesn't do any of these things.

Put a dollar in the basket of the business that you would want to buy from based on what I just told you about each of them.

Now I want to give you a chance to tell me which business you like the best. Raise your hands if you like (or would invest in) Business A. Let me count the hands. Raise your hands if you like (or would invest in) Business B. Raise your hands if you like (or would invest in) Business C.

I asked you earlier, "Does it matter where you spend your money?" Let's look at Business A. Business A puts money into your community. So those of you who put your money into Business A and said you would support it will receive some money back through Business A's community support—let's say 50 percent. (Explain how each of the examples translates in direct resources to the children.) So those who chose Business A get 50 percent of the money that people put in the baskets. Let's figure out how much that would be. People investing in Business A get _____ resources/dollars.

Let's look at Business B. Business B supports the community but not as much and not as directly. Those who supported Business B receive 25 percent of the money back. Let's figure out how much that would be. People investing in Business B get _____ resources/dollars.

Let's look at Business C. Business C does nothing for the community. Since Business C keeps all its money for the company, those of you who selected Business C get no money or resources back.

This lesson features *I Promise*, written by LeBron James and illustrated by Nina Mata. This book embodies the essential values we should all strive to live by: to speak with kindness, to work hard, to help others, to always do our best, and to stay true to ourselves. It is recommended for grades K–4. Guidelines are provided to support students at different levels of reading ability. Discussion questions will connect key concepts from the book to contemporary issues students may encounter in their homes and communities.

Now we're going to read about a superstar who makes a whole lot of money and invests it back in communities like ELEVATE! Show a picture of LeBron James and ask the class, "Do you recognize this person?"

- What is his name?

- What does he do?

- Is he wealthy?

- What are some of the things that LeBron does with his wealth? Does he give time and money to children? Does he give time and money to children who want to learn? Does he give time and money to children who look like you?

Show a picture of LeBron James at his I Promise School.

LeBron James, through his foundation, created the I Promise School. The I Promise School educates students who are falling behind and in danger of falling through the cracks. LeBron said his I Promise School is his greatest accomplishment.

What kinds of things do you think they teach at the I Promise School? Together let's read LeBron's story, *I Promise*.

Look at the cover of the book.

- What do you like most about the cover's picture?

- What are the kids in the picture doing?

- Do they look happy, sad, angry?

Read the story to your students, integrate student readers as appropriate, or access the following read-along option on YouTube: "I PROMISE | Storytime with LeBron and Nina."

We Grow Together

DISCUSSION QUESTIONS: I PROMISE

➡ Do you think LeBron is describing his I Promise School? Why or why not?

➡ Do you think that LeBron is using this book to show us what kinds of promises we should make as ELEVATE! superstars? Why or why not?

➡ What kinds of promises do students make in the story?

➡ What do you think it means to "respect the game plan"? What is the ELEVATE! game plan?

➡ What do you think LeBron means by "run full court"? How can we run full court in ELEVATE!?

➡ What do you think LeBron meant when he said, "Let my magic shine"? How can you let your magic shine at ELEVATE!? At home? At school?

➡ What other promises does the book mention that we also make at ELEVATE!?

CLOSING REFLECTIONS

In sports sometimes we like some teams and players better than others. Some of us don't like sports at all. Whether you like LeBron James or the team he plays for or not, we can respect that he donates his time and money to aid educators like me help children like you learn. And he does more than donate money. He uses his influence as a celebrity to make it cool to be a nice person, a good student, and a helpful person.

We Strive Together

Below, the focus is broken down by grade level.

Lesson plans will include ELEVATE! Wise Words. The Wise Words vocabulary will be connected to the reading lesson designed to build language skills and help students meet Common Core benchmarks. At this point we start building on vocabulary and linking it back to the story—in addition to reinforcing phonetic concepts introduced in previous units.

"One area the ELEVATE! after-school program really brings relevance to is the students' cultural awareness. To truly make young men and young women, especially minorities, culturally aware of their ancestry, where they come from, and where they stand today builds confidence and community" (Dr. Romules Durant, superintendent of Toledo Public Schools).

Kindergartners: With prompting and support, compare and contrast the adventures and experiences of characters in familiar stories (in this case, we're comparing *I Promise* to ELEVATE!), name the author and illustrator of a story and define the role of each in telling the story, describe the relationship between illustrations and the text in which they appear (e.g., what person, place, thing, or idea in the text an illustration depicts), and identify the reasons an author gives to support points in a text.[34]

First Graders: The goal for first graders is to use the illustrations and details in a text to describe its key ideas, identify the reasons an author gives to support points in a text, and identify basic similarities and differences between two texts on the same topic (e.g., in illustrations, descriptions, or procedures). Additionally encourage range of reading and level of text complexity with prompts and support for the student to read informational texts appropriately complex for grade 1 and encourage craft and structure knowledge through the identification of words and phrases in stories or poems that suggest feelings or appeal to the senses.[35]

> "One area the ELEVATE! after-school program really brings relevance to is the students' cultural awareness. To truly make young men and young women, especially minorities, culturally aware of their ancestry, where they come from, and where they stand today builds confidence and community" **(Dr. Romules Durant, superintendent of Toledo Public Schools).**

---

34   Common Core State Standards Initiative, "English Language Arts Standards," accessed September 3, 2021, http://www.corestandards.org/ELA-Literacy/RL/K/.

35   Ibid., accessed September 3, 2021, http://www.corestandards.org/ELA-Literacy/RL/1/.

Second Graders: The goal is to describe how characters in a story respond to major events and challenges and identify the main purpose of a text, including what the author wants to answer, explain, or describe so that by the end of the year they can read and comprehend literature, including stories and poetry, in the grades 2–3 text complexity band proficiently, with scaffolding as needed at the high end of the range.[36]

Third Graders: The goal is to read with sufficient accuracy and fluency to support comprehension, read grade-level text with purpose and understanding, distinguish their own point of view from that of the narrator or of the characters, and determine the meaning of words and phrases as they are used in a text, distinguishing literal from nonliteral language.[37]

WISE WORDS

General Vocabulary

➡ Community

➡ Wealth

➡ Giving Back

I Promise Vocabulary

Grades K–1	Grades 2–3
School	Promise
Read	Leader
Magic	Questions
Change	Believe
Elders	
Courageous	

---

36   Ibid., accessed September 3, 2021, http://www.corestandards.org/ELA-Literacy/RL/2/.

37   Ibid., accessed September 3, 2021, http://www.corestandards.org/ELA-Literacy/RL/3/.

We Work Together

This is where we allow students to expand the lesson beyond the book and apply other types of intelligence and experiences. In this activity students will design their own athletic jersey and then hypothetically share how much they would sell their jersey for, what portion of the proceeds they would donate to their community, and who they would donate those proceeds to in order to affirm the concepts of community, wealth, and giving back.

While students work on their projects, tap into one or more of the songs from ELEVATE!'s music library (https://app.sellwire.net/p/2GA) related to this lesson: "ELEVATE!," "ELEVATE! Affirmation," "ELEVATE! Superstars," "Children of Royalty," "When I Win, We Win."

MATERIALS

T-shirt for each child, fabric paint, pencils with brand-new erasers on top, stencils in different shapes (for example, athletic logos, hearts, or other shapes that students like), and stenciled numbers (for the back of the jersey).

INSTRUCTIONS

Each child should have their own t-shirt, fabric paint, and pencil. They should choose a shape for the front of their jersey and numbers for the back. Each child should dip the eraser in the fabric paint and create dots with the painted eraser around each stencil.

COLLABORATIVE GROUP ACTIVITY

Each student should have time to share their jersey. To expand the activity, each child can tell the group what price they would sell the jersey for, the portion of the proceeds they would donate to their community, and whom they would donate the proceeds to.

CONCLUSION

You all made some awesome jerseys today. I am impressed with the causes you chose to donate your proceeds to. Please keep in mind that, like LeBron, success is about more than talent. It's about sticking to the rules of the game. Before we conclude today, please share one thing that you promise to do to make you a better ELEVATE! student and an ELEVATE! superstar.

We Rise Together

This is the point where you and the students review the progress for the day or the week and reinforce the lessons and unit focus. It's time to lead them in affirming their progress!

"ELEVATE! SUPERSTARS"

➡ [Child's name, group name, or the entire Class] is a superstar.

➡ [Child's achievement] makes [her/him/them] a superstar.

➡ Keep shooting for the stars.

➡ We love to watch you *elevate*!

Additional Resources

Songs from the ELEVATE! music library
(https://app.sellwire.net/p/2GA):

"ELEVATE!"

"ELEVATE! Affirmation"

"ELEVATE! Superstars"

"Children of Royalty"

"When I Win, We Win"

I Promise School

"NAAM's Interactive Story Time: Madam C. J. Walker Builds a Business"

UNIT 5

ELEVATING EXPRESSION

Don't let anyone rob you of your imagination, your creativity, or your curiosity. Go on and do all you can with it and make it the life you want to live.

—MAE JEMISON, MD, ASTRONAUT, AND FIRST AFRICAN AMERICAN WOMAN IN SPACE

ARE WE PROVIDING our students with a broad enough experience to be able to connect with their passions, purpose, and potential career paths early enough, or is our teaching biased toward specific skills and talents that limit personal pursuits and career options? Are we doing enough to encourage Black children to embrace the expressiveness embedded in the African culture? These are the questions that drive the holistic approach of the ELEVATE! program. The curriculum speaks to the whole child, opening their eyes to all their unique skills and talents and how those can translate into a wide range of future pursuits.

By now you have observed the expression of your students' creativity through the We Work Together projects in units 1 through 4. What new talents did you notice? How did your affirmation of those talents affect the students, and how will you help those students connect their unique gifts to real-life learning and goals?

In every lesson, a wide variety of creative skills can be connected to traditional academic subjects like math and language. You saw in unit 2, lesson 1 the incorporation of math, reading, expression, and language skills through the children's collaborative efforts in making the "Children of Royalty" video. In the same way, cooking projects connect math through measurement and timing, and it connects language through recipes. Drawing projects can tie in math by introducing scaling. And guess what? Through these creative activities, the mathematically sound child may never learn how to draw, but they may become more cognizant of color or more appreciative of art or the construct. Creative expression opens the path for those who are naturally inclined toward creativity and those who are not. It is not intended to "make" all children artists but to expand every student's horizon of their unique gifts and value and all that is possible for them as individuals and for their communities.

A. Wade Boykin, professor and director of the graduate program in the Department of Psychology at Howard University, and Forrest D. Toms, former associate professor at North Carolina Agricultural and Technical State University, in their article "Black Child Socialization: A Conceptual Framework," identified nine cultural dimensions common to African culture that they observed being expressed through the behavioral patterns and values of African American families. Of those nine principles, four (45 percent) are connected to creativity and expression. They are identified as the following:

Movement—approaching life rhythmically, particularly as expressed through the patterned, interwoven mosaic of music, movement, and percussiveness.

Affect—a premium placed on emotional sensibilities and expressiveness.

Expressive individualism—a premium attached to the cultivation of distinctiveness, spontaneity, and uniqueness of self-expression.

Orality—a special emphasis on oral and aural modes of communication, especially the use of the spoken word to convey deep textural meanings not possible through the written word.

Curtain Call

At one of our recent student showcases, a group of boys chose to perform a song. Now these boys were not musically inclined, but they didn't realize that, and they worked hard, and they gave it their best. Their performance had its challenges, but the boys were fully invested in it. They were so into their routine that they were oblivious to the recommendations of other nurturing staff and adults. The dads in the audience were taken aback, surprised by the unexpected sight and sound of their sons belting out a song. They were falling over in their chairs, laughing at their sons' performance.

Once the boys were finished and off the stage, I took the mic, and I said, "Listen, how many ten-year-old Black boys do you know that would be brave enough to get up and do what your sons just did? Now what do you think your laughing at them tells them?" I reminded them that their words and their responses matter and that we don't want to send the message that we think our kids should be ashamed for trying their best even if it wasn't great. *We want to affirm them when they are brave, when they are creative, when they dare to express feelings and emotions.* Laughing at them tells them to be ashamed of putting themselves out there and taking a chance, and I reminded them that we don't do that at ELEVATE! Once presented in this way, the dads' attitudes shifted, and they began to clap for their sons, affirming that the fact that their boys sang in front of a crowd of two hundred took courage.

As educators we are responsible for the encouragement and support of our students in our school community. We are also the creators and caretakers of our school community, and we must hold all members who enter our community accountable to the standards we have set. In this unit you'll share the story of Beyoncé and how, through perseverance, she was able to express herself creatively and share it with the world.

LESSON 5: UNLEASHING MY EXPRESSION

. . . .

We Shine Together

Lead children in the expression of daily affirmations, allowing each child to recite individually:

"Today I feel _____

_____

_____."

"I can make my day better by _____

_____

_____."

"I can help make _____'s day

better by _____

_____

_____."

Together sing the "ELEVATE! Affirmation" song. Beginning each lesson with this song allows you, the teacher, to set the cultural tone for the classroom—a tone that tells the students that everyone is welcome and that each and every child will be loved and accepted for their unique traits and abilities.

Mathematicians and artists,

Musicians and lyricists,

They are all gifts;

They are loved at ELEVATE!

Athletes and readers,

Supporters and leaders,

All kinds of believers

Are loved at ELEVATE!

Hair kinky or straight,

Long tresses or a fade,

Eyes of all shapes

Are loved at ELEVATE!

Fair skin

To every shade of melanin,

We are all kin;

You are loved at ELEVATE!

A temperament that's mild

Or with a little bit of spice,

Personas of all types

Are loved at ELEVATE!;

At ELEVATE!,

Everybody can find their place.

Never have to worry about feeling hate,

Everybody's loved at ELEVATE!

We Learn Together

The "Elevating Expression" curriculum addresses the concepts of expression, creativity, and perseverance, demonstrating the many ways a person can be creative and the importance of believing in yourself and a willingness to work hard to make your dreams come true. Write the words *expression*, *creativity*, and *perseverance* on the board as you discuss each.

EXPRESSION

→ Have you heard of the word *expression*?

→ Where have you heard the word *expression*?

→ Who can put the word *expression* in a sentence?

→ What do you think it means to have expression?

→ What does it mean to be expressive?

→ In what ways do you express yourself? You can express yourself through talking, smiling, frowning, writing, painting, how you dress, and so much more.

→ How you express yourself is unique to you. (Remember how we talked about *unique* in our "Elevating Confidence" unit? Do you remember what it means?)

→ You can express yourself in creative ways.

CREATIVITY

→ Have you heard of the word *creativity*?

→ Where have you heard the word *creativity*?

→ Who can put the word *creativity* in a sentence?

➡ What do you think it means to have creativity?

➡ What does it mean to be creative?

➡ In what ways are you creative?

PERSEVERANCE

➡ Have you ever heard of the word *perseverance*?

➡ Where have you heard the word *perseverance*?

➡ Do you remember learning to read your first book? First, you had to learn the alphabet and all the different sounds that the letters make, then you had to learn how to put letters together to make a word, and then you had to learn what all those words mean. After doing all that, you could begin to learn to read your first sentence. Learning to read a book can be hard, and it can take a long time—but you persevered and did it.

CREATIVITY ACTIVITY

Now we're going to do a short activity about *expression* and the many ways that we can engage through it.

Let's pull out our red, yellow, and green cards. On the screen I will show you some activities. If you think it's a way to express yourself, then put up your green card. If you don't think it's a way to express yourself, then put up your red card. If you're not sure, use your yellow card.

• Doing your homework

• Acting on a stage

• Painting a picture

- Figure skating

- Dancing

- Designing clothing

- Cooking

- Singing

- Writing a story

Guess what? You can use your own unique expression to do *all* these things. Today we're going to focus on expression through music. What types of music do you like? Use your cards (green, red, and yellow) to tell us if you like it, don't like it, or are unsure.

- Rap

- Rhythm and blues

- Rock and roll

- Neo soul

- Country

- Inspirational

Now it's your turn to be expressive. Each one of you is going to write a line to a song. (Note: For students in younger grades, it may work best to work in small groups. Each student/group needs to pick a music genre that they like. Teachers should order stock music from firms like AudioJungle so that the child can add their lyrics and tune accordingly.)

Here's the template:

My name is _____, they know me near and far, because I'm an ELEVATE! superstar!

I [an attribute the child likes about themselves], so I *know* I'm great! I'm going to be a(n) [desired career], watch me *ELEVATE!*

Remember your song so you can present it to the group during craft time.

This lesson features *Beyoncé: Shine Your Light*, written by Sarah E. Warren and illustrated by Geneva Bowers. Written for children in grades K–3, *Beyoncé: Shine Your Light* is the biography of a superstar in the making. A shy, soft-spoken little girl, Beyoncé found her voice through song, unleashing her expression and emboldening her to become the beautiful, amazing, and talented woman she is today.

Guidelines are provided to support students at different levels of reading ability. Discussion questions will connect key concepts from the book to contemporary issues students may encounter in their homes and communities.

Look at the cover of the book *Beyoncé: Shine Your Light*.

- Does anyone recognize this woman?

- What do you think this story might be about?

- What do you know about Beyoncé?

Read the story to your students, integrate student readers as appropriate, or access the following read-along option on the Sankofa Read Aloud YouTube channel.

We Grow Together

DISCUSSION QUESTIONS: BEYONCÉ: SHINE YOUR LIGHT

➡ How old was Beyoncé when she began singing and performing? (Be sure to integrate pictures that demonstrate the answers to this question.)

Supplementary information

- Beyoncé won her first talent show at age seven.
- Beyoncé performed with her singing group on a national TV show, *Star Search*, at age twelve.
- She earned her first record deal before she became an adult.

➡ Did the young Beyoncé always act like a performer? Was she always loud and on a stage? Was she shy? Why do you think she was so quiet?

➡ Did Beyoncé become successful all on her own? Who helped her? How did she receive that help?

➡ Was all of Beyoncé's creative *expression* natural, or did she have to work at it too? How hard did she work?

➡ Have people always appreciated the ways in which she expressed herself? Did she give up, or did she *persevere*?

➡ Beyoncé's group lost on *Star Search* (in the story).

Supplementary information

- The record company signed Beyoncé and her group and then dropped them.
- Two of Beyoncé's group members quit the group.

➡ Beyoncé persevered even when things were hard, and because of that, she won a lot of awards.

Supplementary information

- Beyoncé has sold over 118 million records and holds twenty-four Grammy Awards.

➡ Does Beyoncé just shine the spotlight on herself, or does she look for ways to shine the spotlight on others too? How?

CLOSING REFLECTIONS

We learned that even though Beyoncé is a confident and successful singer today, she was very shy and didn't have a lot of confidence when she was a young girl. But once Beyoncé discovered she could sing, her voice and her confidence grew stronger, and she found many ways to *express* her creativity. In what other ways, besides singing and dancing, does Beyoncé communicate with her fans?

- She has developed clothing lines.

- She owns an entertainment company, which means she can run businesses and has to use math skills.

- She writes songs and lyrics, which means that she not only has musical talent but also uses language arts and reading skills.

As we close this lesson, let's remember that music and performing are ways to express yourself in your own unique way, but they are not the only ways. We need to also remember that performing is not just about singing and dancing, because to be able to sing and dance you need to learn how to read and count. And no matter how you unleash your expression, it is important to take time to be still and quiet so that you can think, dream, and create more. And being a star is not easy, nor is being an ELEVATE! superstar. Like Beyoncé you must learn to listen, work hard, and succeed and then use that success to help others and develop your expression in new ways.

We Strive Together

Lesson plans will include ELEVATE! Wise Words. The Wise Words vocabulary will be connected to the reading lesson designed to build language skills and help students meet Common Core benchmarks. At this point, in addition to reinforcing phonetic concepts introduced in previous units, we will begin building on vocabulary and linking it back to the story.

Below, the focus is broken down by grade level.

"What I like best about the Center of Hope is that everyone is really nice, and they always try to teach me new things and help me with the things I don't know" (Bella Cutcher, ELEVATE! student).

Kindergartners: With prompting and support, ask and answer questions about key details in a text. Identify characters, settings, and major events in a story. Ask and answer questions about unknown words in a text.[38]

First Graders: Ask and answer questions about key details in a text. Describe characters, settings, and major events in a story using key details.[39]

Second Graders: Identify the main purpose of a text, including what the author wants to answer, explain, or describe. Describe how characters in a story respond to major events and challenges. By the end of the year, read and comprehend literature, including stories and poetry, in the grades 2–3 text complexity band proficiently, with scaffolding as needed at the high end of the range.[40]

Third Graders: Describe characters in a story (e.g., their traits, motivations, or feelings) and explain how their actions contribute to the sequence of

> "What I like best about the Center of Hope is that everyone is really nice, and they always try to teach me new things and help me with the things I don't know" **(Bella Cutcher, ELEVATE! student).**

---

38   Ibid., accessed September 3, 2021, http://www.corestandards.org/ELA-Literacy/RL/K/1/ and http://www.corestandards.org/ELA-Literacy/RL/K/3/.

39   Ibid., accessed September 3, 2021, http://www.corestandards.org/ELA-Literacy/RL/1/1/ and http://www.corestandards.org/ELA-Literacy/RL/1/3/.

40   Ibid., accessed September 3, 2021, http://www.corestandards.org/ELA-Literacy/RI/2/6/ and http://www.corestandards.org/ELA-Literacy/RI/2/10/.

events. Refer to parts of stories, dramas, and poems when writing or speaking about a text using terms such as *chapter*, *scene*, and *stanza*; describe how each successive part builds on earlier sections.[41]

WISE WORDS

General Vocabulary

➡ Expression

➡ Creativity

➡ Perseverance

Beyoncé Shine Your Light Vocabulary

Grades K–1	Grades 2–3
Quiet	Onstage
Fierce	Performed
Goofy	Designing
Angry	Independent
Regal	Styling
	Coaching
	Gigantic
	Inspired

---

41   Ibid., accessed September 3, 2021, http://www.corestandards.org/ELA-Literacy/RL/3/3/ and http://www.corestandards.org/ELA-Literacy/RL/3/5/.

We Work Together

This is where we allow students to expand the lesson beyond the book and apply other types of intelligence and experiences. This lesson's art/craft project enhances each student's unique expression by creating an album cover.

While students work on their projects, tap into one or more of the songs from ELEVATE!'s music library (https://app.sellwire.net/p/2GA) related to this lesson: "ELEVATE!," "ELEVATE! Affirmation," "ELEVATE! Superstars," "Watch Me ELEVATE!."

MATERIALS

CD sleeves or cases, black poster board cut into circles, two aluminum foil circles per child, smaller poster board circles cut in white (to design the inside of the CD or album), scissors, glue, markers/colored pencils.

INSTRUCTIONS

Each child should have either a CD sleeve or a CD case with a blank insert. They should select a title with the word *elevate* in it for the song they created in the opening activity. Each child should design their CD sleeve or case. Then they should glue the two foil circles onto the front and back of the black poster board circle so that it resembles a CD. Then on the smaller white poster board circle, they should design that and glue it in the middle. When it dries, they can put the CD into the sleeve or the case. This can be adapted to be an album cover with poster board glued/stapled around three sides. Larger black circles can be cut to resemble records instead of CDs.

COLLABORATIVE GROUP ACTIVITY

Each student should have time to share their album and their song. Teachers should prompt them to reference the genre they chose and why they chose it. Integrate math into this activity by asking the children how much they would sell their song for and how many CDs/records they would have to sell to earn a certain amount of money. For older students the cost of production could be added to calculate profit.

CONCLUSION

We used a lot of skills today. We used literacy and visual arts, and we performed our songs. We learned about an interesting woman who worked very hard and faced some challenges before she became successful. How did Beyoncé do that? She *persevered*. It is through *expression* that we find our uniqueness and are able to put our special mark on this earth.

We Rise Together

This is the point where you and the students review the progress for the day or the week and reinforce the lessons and unit focus. It's time to lead them in affirming their progress!

"ELEVATE! SUPERSTARS"

➡ [Child's name, group name, or the entire class] is a superstar.

➡ [Child's achievement] makes [her/him/them] a superstar.

➡ Keep shooting for the stars.

➡ We love to watch you *elevate*!

Additional Resources

Songs from the ELEVATE! music library
(https://app.sellwire.net/p/2GA):

"ELEVATE!"

"ELEVATE! Affirmation"

"ELEVATE! Superstars"

"Watch Me ELEVATE!"

BeyGood Foundation website

ELEVATING INTO OUR FUTURE

Surely humans were chosen to bring good into the world.

—ANCIENT TEACHINGS OF THE ODU IFA

GUIDING STUDENTS INTO their future is a tremendous responsibility. At varying times in our lives, many of us as adults require guidance on that quest. I was halfway through my MBA when I began questioning how my purpose would lead me into my future. My friends had begun graduating, entering the corporate world, and making all kinds of money. Watching them I realized that I didn't desire any of that. It then became clear to me that my purpose for the future was to share my gifts to teach, encourage, and *elevate* children, in particular Black children.

The key to guiding a child on their path to their future is listening and observing—listening to what matters and what is relevant to them individually, culturally, and familially and observing what their gifts and skills are—and then helping them develop the tools needed to determine where they want to go and how they want to get there. Benson's 40 Developmental Assets model of the Positive Youth Development framework correlates a youth's optimism for the future and sense of purpose with lower levels of multiple risk behaviors and higher levels of thriving regardless of gender, ethnicity, socioeconomic status, and geographic residence. The development of a positive identity requires an individual sense of purpose and a positive view of one's personal future.[42]

The research of Stanford education professor William Damon confirms that we seek purpose at varying times in our lives and that to find purpose we must find something meaningful that we desire to accomplish in conjunction with a willingness to take action and do the work necessary to fulfill it.[43] Young children require significant support and direction, and therefore, much of what they accomplish is done so out of obligation to an adult's request rather than a sense of personal meaning. They also often lack the skills and knowledge to pursue their purpose on their own, but with guidance children can develop meaningful pursuits and the skills and knowledge to reach for them.

Damon shares two key realizations that set young people on the path to finding their purpose: the realizations that a need exists in the world that requires action (for a young child, that purpose may be an awareness that the new kid in class is shy and needs a friend or that when they play with their baby brother or sister, their mom is able to get things done) and that they, as an individual, are capable of affecting change (i.e., the new kid in class is smiling more, or their

---

42   D. T. Shek et al., "Positive Youth Development: Current Perspectives," Adolescent Health, Medicine, and Therapeutics 10 (2019): 131–41, https://doi.org/10.2147/AHMT.S179946.

43   Clifton B. Parker, "Sense of Youthful Purpose Driven by Action, Passion, Says Stanford Researcher," Stanford News, April 14, 2015, https://news.stanford.edu/2015/04/14/purpose-youth-damon-041415/.

mom said she really appreciated their help with the baby). A strong sense of self, a belief that we are all interconnected, and a willingness to cooperate collectively for the greater good all aid in discovering one's purpose.

Singing into the Future

Recognizing a child's gift and helping them tap into that gift to find their purpose for their future can have a profound impact on their attitude and behavior. One student I taught struggled to behave and participate in class, always creating a disruption to garner the attention of her classmates. One day she had to wait behind before going to gym because of her behavior. When she pulled herself together, she and I began to walk down the hall to gym. Just a few steps in and beside me, I hear this sweet voice singing, "We have the power."

I stopped immediately and asked, "Did you know you can really sing?"

She said, "No."

"Well, you *can* really sing."

I coached her on her singing, and soon her mom was taking her to sing in church pageants more than fifty miles away. This student's mom supported her daughter's passion and found her opportunities to share her gift. Guess what happened next? The behavioral issues disappeared.

In this unit you'll provide your students with a curriculum that draws on the components of units 1, 2, and 3 to help them understand how they can have agency in their future and begin to identify their individual purpose that will lead them there.

LESSON 6: REACHING FOR MY POTENTIAL

We Shine Together

Lead children in the expression of daily affirmations, allowing each child to recite individually:

"Today I feel _____

_____

_____."

"I can make my day better by _____

_____

_____."

"I can help make _____'s day

better by _____

_____

_____."

Together sing the "ELEVATE! Affirmation" song. Beginning each lesson with this song allows you, the teacher, to set the cultural tone for the classroom—a tone that tells the students that everyone is welcome and that each and every child will be loved and accepted for their unique traits and abilities.

Mathematicians and artists,

Musicians and lyricists,

They are all gifts;

They are loved at ELEVATE!

Athletes and readers,

Supporters and leaders,

All kinds of believers

Are loved at ELEVATE!

Hair kinky or straight,

Long tresses or a fade,

Eyes of all shapes

Are loved at ELEVATE!

Fair skin

To every shade of melanin,

We are all kin;

You are loved at ELEVATE!

A temperament that's mild

Or with a little bit of spice,

Personas of all types

Are loved at ELEVATE!;

At ELEVATE!,

Everybody can find their place.

Never have to worry about feeling hate,

Everybody's loved at ELEVATE!

We Learn Together

In our time together, we've talked about how important it is to have confidence, treat one another like family, and express ourselves in creative ways and how each one of us is an important part of the ELEVATE! circle. You are important to this circle, to your school, to your family, and to your community. Each one of you brings value to ELEVATE! You are a *superstar*. What you do, how you act, and the choices you make can elevate you into your future.

Write the words *future*, *purpose*, *special*, and *contribution* on the board as you discuss each.

FUTURE

- ➡ Have you heard of the word *future*?
- ➡ Where have you heard the word *future*?
- ➡ Who can put the word *future* in a sentence?
- ➡ Can you see your future?
- ➡ Can you have dreams for your future?
- ➡ Can you make choices that help you reach the future you want?

PURPOSE

- ➡ What do you think *purpose* means?
- ➡ What does it mean to have purpose?
- ➡ When have you felt a special purpose for doing something?

SPECIAL

- ➡ Have you ever heard of the word *special*?

➡ Where have you heard the word *special?*

➡ What do you think *special* means?

CONTRIBUTION

➡ Have you ever heard of the word *contribution?*

➡ Where have you heard the word *contribution?*

➡ What do you think *contribution* means?

INTO OUR FUTURE DISCUSSION

Your purpose is even bigger than a goal, and it is what helps lead you into your future. Your purpose is your reason for being on this earth. Your purpose is the reason you set certain goals.

Why is it important to think about your future?

➡ Do you believe you can decide what your future will be? Why or why not?

➡ If you know some of the things you want to do in your future, what steps can you take to help make those things happen?

➡ When you see your future, you are more likely to set goals and reach them.

Why is it important to have a purpose?

➡ When you feel like your life has purpose, you are more likely to make positive choices because you don't want anything to stop you from fulfilling your purpose for being here on the earth. And because, in ELEVATE!, we have spent weeks talking and sharing about why you are important, why you are valued, and why you are a superstar, each one of you should feel confident in finding your purpose. Because you know that you are a superstar, your purpose should aim *beyond the stars*.

Do you have to be a grown-up to think about and plan for your future? Let's see.

(Display images of Yolanda Renee King, daughter of Martin Luther King III; Naomi Wadler with March for Our Lives; and the Birmingham Children's Crusade.)

➡ Are the people in these pictures/videos grown-ups?

➡ What does it look like they're doing?

➡ Where do you think they might be?

➡ What do you think their hope for their future and that of others might be?

➡ Is it easy to figure out what you want to do in the future? It's not always easy, but you can start by thinking about all the things we talked about in "Elevating Confidence," "Elevating Our Circle," "Elevating Cooperation," "Elevating Community," and "Elevating Expression."

    ▫ What are the things you like to do?

    ▫ What are the things you want to learn to do?

    ▫ What are your unique qualities that make you special?

    ▫ Now think about how you can use the things you like to do and the things that make you uniquely you to elevate your family, friends, classmates, school, and communities through sharing, cooperation, and giving back. What will your future look like when you do that?

Today we are going to talk about a little girl whose goal was just to go to school. By going to a particular school, even though no one wanted her there, she changed what her future and that of many children would be. I know that our ELEVATE! superstars will be able to help me figure out how this little girl changed her future. As you listen I want you to think about what kind of story this might be.

- Have you heard the word *fiction*?

- Who knows what *fiction* means?

- Have you ever heard the word *nonfiction*?

- Who knows what *nonfiction* means?

- As we read this story, see how quickly you can figure out if this story is fiction or nonfiction.

This lesson features *The Story of Ruby Bridges*, written by Robert Coles and illustrated by George Ford. This is the true story of how, through her own strength and her family's love and faith, Ruby Bridges changed history by daring to go to a school where many people didn't think she belonged. It is recommended for grades K–3. Guidelines are provided to support students at different levels of reading ability. Discussion questions will connect key concepts from the book to contemporary issues students may encounter in their homes and communities.

Look at the cover of the book *The Story of Ruby Bridges*.

- Have you ever heard of Ruby Bridges?

- What do you think this story might be about?

- Where do you think Ruby is going?

- Why do you think the people in the background look so angry?

Read the story to your students, integrate student readers as appropriate, or access the following read-along option on the Mr. Alicea's Arcade of Knowledge YouTube channel.

If there is a concern about religiosity in this version, *Ruby Bridges Goes to School: My True Story* can be substituted. You can find the read-along version on the Sankofa Read Aloud YouTube channel.

We Grow Together

DISCUSSION QUESTIONS: THE STORY OF RUBY BRIDGES

➡ What was the main character's name?

➡ Was this a true story? If so, was it fiction or nonfiction?

➡ What was the problem in the story?

➡ How do you think Ruby felt?

➡ What types of challenges did Ruby face?

➡ How did she handle those challenges?

➡ Was it easy for Ruby to stay focused? Why or why not?

➡ How do you think you would have handled those challenges?

➡ What special contributions did Ruby make to our country?

➡ How might Ruby's future be different if she had run away from her purpose?

➡ Ruby's family was very religious. However, there are ways to follow Ruby's example, even if you don't believe in her specific faith. If we are not religious, we can send positive thoughts and intentions to those who stand in the way of us achieving the future we want for ourselves.

➡ How has Ruby continued changing the future?

➡ Do you have to be an adult to have a vision for your future? Do you have to be rich or have a fancy title to make a contribution that changes the future?

CLOSING REFLECTIONS

When Ruby was a little girl, she had to do something really hard just so she could get the education she deserved. Ruby was too little to understand that she was contributing to the future of Black children in America, but her parents knew, and they supported her and loved her and had faith in her so that she could give hope that the future would be better and brighter for everyone. Ruby came to understand her purpose when she got older and has spent her life advocating for civil rights. Today Ruby says, "I believe that when you accept the work of civil rights, it's not a job. It's a calling."[44]

We Strive Together

Lesson plans will include ELEVATE! Wise Words. The Wise Words vocabulary will be connected to the reading lesson designed to build language skills and help students meet Common Core benchmarks. At this point we continue building on vocabulary and linking it back to the story—in addition to reinforcing phonetic concepts introduced in previous units. Below, the focus is broken down by grade level.

"The Center of Hope is a high-performing organization. I admire their courage to raise their hands and be willing to examine whether they are truly impactful to their community. Our research

---

44 Nicolle Carroll, "Ruby Bridges Was Six When She Walked into a Segregated School. Now She Teaches Children to Get Past Racial Differences," Life, USA Today, August 12, 2020, https://www.usatoday.com/in-depth/life/women-of-the-century/2020/08/12/19th-amendment-ruby-bridges-now-teaches-kids-racism-and-peace/5555100002/.

shows they are!" (Sheri Jones, former deputy director of performance evaluations for Franklin County, Ohio).

Kindergartners: With prompting and support, be able to ask and answer questions about key details in a text. Be able to ask and answer questions about unknown words in a text.[45]

First Graders: Be able to ask and answer questions about key details in a text and describe characters, settings, and major events in a story using key details.[46]

Second Graders: Be able to ask and answer such questions as *who, what, where, when, why,* and *how* to demonstrate understanding of key details in a text.[47]

Third Graders: Be able to describe the overall structure of a story, including describing how the beginning introduces the story and how the ending concludes the action, and be able to describe how characters in a story respond to major events and challenges.[48]

> "The Center of Hope is a high-performing organization. I admire their courage to raise their hands and be willing to examine whether they are truly impactful to their community. Our research shows they are!" (Sheri Jones, former deputy director of performance evaluations for Franklin County, Ohio).

---

45   Common Core State Standards Initiative, "English Language Arts Standards," accessed September 3, 2021, http://www.corestandards.org/ELA-Literacy/RI/K/1/ and http://www.corestandards.org/ELA-Literacy/RI/K/4/.

46   Ibid., accessed September 3, 2021, http://www.corestandards.org/ELA-Literacy/RL/1/1/ and http://www.corestandards.org/ELA-Literacy/RL/1/3/.

47   Ibid., accessed September 3, 2021, http://www.corestandards.org/ELA-Literacy/RI/2/1/.

48   Ibid., accessed September 3, 2021, http://www.corestandards.org/ELA-Literacy/RL/3/5/ and http://www.corestandards.org/ELA-Literacy/RL/3/3/.

WISE WORDS

General Vocabulary

➡ Future

➡ Purpose

➡ Special

➡ Contribution

➡ Fiction

➡ Nonfiction

The Story of Ruby Bridges Vocabulary

Grades K–1	Grades 2–3
Cabin	Nation
Fair	Children
Grade	Judge
Proud	Marshals
Love	Chosen
Crowd	Law
	Courage
	Faith

We Work Together

This is where we allow students to expand the lesson beyond the book and apply other types of intelligence and experiences. This lesson's focus is on *elevating* into our future.

While students work on their projects, tap into one or more of the songs from ELEVATE!'s music library (https://app.sellwire. net/p/2GA) related to this lesson: "ELEVATE!," "ELEVATE! Affirmation," "ELEVATE! Superstars," "Children of Royalty," "When I Win, We Win," "Watch Me ELEVATE!," "It's Our Time."

MATERIALS

Poster board for each child, stencils (alphabet, arch, circles, and varied sizes of stars), construction paper, a picture of each child, assorted pictures of African Americans who have careers or a calling that the students emulate, scissors, glue, and markers. Make sure each picture of an African American figure has a caption with the person's name and how they became influential.

INSTRUCTIONS

Each child should trace and cut out letters that say, "Elevating into my future," and "Aiming above the stars." For younger students, the letters can be precut. Have students glue "Elevating into my future" at the top and "Aiming above the stars" at the bottom. The child's picture should be in the bottom left corner, enclosed in a circle. The picture of the person they aspire to be like (or who has a similar purpose) should be at the top right corner, encased in a circle. In the arch the student (or teacher with student guidance) should write, "My purpose for the future is to _____, like [the person they selected to emulate]."

COLLABORATIVE GROUP ACTIVITY

Assist students in distinguishing a person's career from their purpose as needed. Each student should have time to share their poster. When the students are sharing, ask questions that prompt them to think about the things they can do now to elevate into their future.

CONCLUSION

We accomplished a lot this week. We talked about some complex topics. We thought about what we want to do in our future when we grow up and how we can do extraordinary things even when we're young like Ruby. Ruby's story happened a long time ago, but people being mistreated still happens today. Many of us have seen someone being mistreated for going to school or when trying to do the right thing. One thing we can learn from Ruby is that the harder the journey, sometimes the bigger the purpose. Hopefully Ruby's story and the people that you included on your posters are an encouragement for you to keep elevating into the future and aiming above the stars.

If time allows, you may want to encourage children to share mistreatment that they have seen or felt and how that made them feel and how they responded.

We Rise Together

This is the point where you and the students review the progress for the day or the week and reinforce the lessons and unit focus. It's time to lead them in affirming their progress!

"ELEVATE! SUPERSTARS"

→ [Child's name, group name, or the entire class] is a superstar.

→ [Child's achievement] makes [her/him/them] a superstar.

→ Keep shooting for the stars.

→ We love to watch you *elevate*!

Additional Resources

Songs from the ELEVATE! music library (https://app.sellwire.net/p/2GA):

"ELEVATE!"

"ELEVATE! Affirmation"

"ELEVATE! Superstars"

"Children of Royalty"

"When I Win, We Win"

"Watch Me ELEVATE!"

"It's Our Time"

Naomi Wadler's speech on YouTube.

Yolanda Renee King's speech on YouTube.

The Children's Crusade of Birmingham on the History Channel.

Interview with Ruby Bridges, August 12, 2020, USA Today.

ELEVATING HOPE

*History has shown us that courage can be contagious
and hope can take on a life of its own.*
—MICHELLE OBAMA

BEING RAISED AS a Black child in America, every day that I went to school, every day that I picked up the newspaper, I was told one way or another what I couldn't do, what I couldn't be, and what was impossible for me to attain based on the color of my skin. It required a whole lot of hope to keep doing the right thing, to keep going to school, to keep studying hard so I could hold on to the expectation that it would all pay off in a meaningful way someday.

When we sell success and hard work to Black children, it's imperative that we recognize and acknowledge that Black children and adolescents can do all the right things; they can go to school, church, and extracurricular activities; and they can be a part of America's armed services and still get maced, abused, and arrested while doing the very things they are supposed to be doing. It takes hope to be able to keep doing the right things—to keep participating, to not get in trouble, to not fight back.

For a Black child in America, it takes constant hope to make good choices every day. It is not enough to hope that our Black children survive, but they must become empowered to live their best lives, feel connected to a supportive community, and have full access to education and enrichment activities that set them on a path to full thriving. All the adults in the lives of Black children must address and acknowledge the racial stereotypes cast upon African Americans and continually affirm the child's true value. Research has shown that when Black children become aware of the negative perspectives on African Americans and those perspectives are mediated by important people in their lives, including parents, peers, and teachers, they become increasingly resilient to these adverse conditions and experience more positive outcomes.[49]

> For a Black child in America, it takes constant hope to make good choices every day.

At the Center of Hope and the ELEVATE! program, we have made hope our central pillar. Hope draws on all the other components you have been working on with your students. For Black children to sustain hope that propels them forward regardless of the adversity we know they will face, they must have a strong sense of confidence; a sense of harmony, belonging, and mattering to their family, school, and peers; a sense of responsibility to themselves and their community to work cooperatively for the greater good; a sense of greater purpose to guide them into their future; creative expression that allows their unique light to shine; and a belief that as they elevate

---

49   American Psychological Association, Task Force on Resilience and Strength in Black Children and Adolescents, "Resilience in African American Children and Adolescents: A Vision for Optimal Development," (Washington, DC, 2008), http://www.apa.org/pi/cyf/resilience.html.

as individuals, they have a responsibility to elevate their community and those around them.

Hope is the answer to *Why try?* By sharing real-life stories of Black people who have faced racially influenced barriers and overcome them, we can instill expectancy in our children that everything is possible, encouraging them to apply it to their own lives and make informed choices beyond those that society dictates they should make.

If We Believe in Children, They Will Believe in Themselves

Through my work with the Center of Hope and ELEVATE!, I have been part of and observed the development of many children's belief in themselves, and I have witnessed the resulting transformation of their lives. Here are just two examples.

We had a student who had flunked the second grade twice. At ELEVATE! he would not do anything. One day my mother took him aside, and she said, "How many times are you going to flunk the second grade? Is this really what you want for yourself, to be ten or eleven years old and still in the second grade? Is this really all that you think you're capable of doing? I believe you can do so much more." This student got his homework caught up, and he passed the second grade that year. I saw him again when he was in the sixth grade, and he was doing well. He had, at some point, finally believed that he was capable of doing the work.

We worked with a group of students in another after-school program to try to bring up their reading level. They would pretend to be asleep, or they would be disruptive the minute you opened a book to read with them. The program was very structured, but the students resisted the structure, and the aides began to believe that the students were incapable of learning.

One of the first lessons I taught was the hope lesson you are about to teach to your students. This lesson is centered on the story of *Hidden Figures: The True Story of Four Black Women and the Space Race*. In addition to showing those students that people who looked like them were pivotal in putting the first human on the moon, I spent time talking about the fact that these smart and capable women weren't allowed to use the same bathrooms as the Whites and that they had to walk far to use *their* bathroom. They also faced discrimination in the cafeteria, having to eat in separate areas and not having access to all the foods that Whites had available to them. We also talked about how even though they provided the challenging mathematical answers that solved many seemingly impossible problems, they were often not given credit or recognized for their contributions. We talked honestly about the inequity and unfairness that happened to those women and their ultimate and incredible success in a field that they loved.

I asked if the women in *Hidden Figures* ran around the room, screaming or throwing things when they couldn't use the bathroom or didn't get the credit they deserved. Then we broke down the constructive, self-respectful approach they did use and how their confidence in their own abilities and their hope for a better future carried them through. We also discussed what they considered to be unfair in their schools and the ways that they could responsibly address them.

We continued to work with those students fifteen hours per week for seven months, integrating each lesson into their everyday lives and connecting the dots. "You love playing video games and may want to create them one day? Guess what? You need to know how to read and do math, and here are people who look like you who create the video games you play." We incorporated reading and math into simple cooking lessons—real-life connections are essential if children are to have *hope* that the work they are putting in will have a benefit in the end. During the period that we worked with the students, children at grade-level reading increased from 32 percent to 60 percent or above.

Everything is possible, but you must believe it is so. In this unit, you'll provide your students with a curriculum based on a true story of four women whose hope enabled them to achieve the impossible.

LESSON 7: LEADING WITH HOPE

We Shine Together

Lead children in the expression of daily affirmations, allowing each child to recite individually:

"Today I feel _____
_____
_____."

"I can make my day better by _____
_____
_____."

"I can help make _____'s day
better by _____
.
_____
_____."

Together sing the "ELEVATE! Affirmation" song. Beginning each lesson with this song allows you, the teacher, to set the cultural tone for the classroom—a tone that tells the students that everyone is welcome and that each and every child will be loved and accepted for their unique traits and abilities.

Mathematicians and artists,

Musicians and lyricists,

They are all gifts;

They are loved at ELEVATE!

Athletes and readers,

Supporters and leaders,

All kinds of believers

Are loved at ELEVATE!

Hair kinky or straight,

Long tresses or a fade,

Eyes of all shapes

Are loved at ELEVATE!

Fair skin

To every shade of melanin,

We are all kin;

You are loved at ELEVATE!

A temperament that's mild

Or with a little bit of spice,

Personas of all types

Are loved at ELEVATE!;

At ELEVATE!,

Everybody can find their place.

Never have to worry about feeling hate,

Everybody's loved at ELEVATE!

We Learn Together

The "Elevating Hope" curriculum addresses the concepts of expectancy that things can and will be better. Through hope we can make the impossible possible. Write the words *impossible*, *hope*, and *representation* on the board as you discuss each.

IMPOSSIBLE

➡ Have you heard of the word *impossible*?

➡ Where have you heard the word *impossible*?

➡ Who can put the word *impossible* in a sentence?

➡ What do you think *impossible* means?

➡ Are there things you think are impossible?

➡ What are they, and why do you think they are impossible to achieve?

HOPE

➡ Have you ever heard of the word *hope*?

➡ Where have you heard the word *hope*?

➡ What do you think *hope* means?

➡ Who can put the word *hope* in a sentence?

REPRESENTATION

➡ Have you ever heard of the word *representation*?

➡ Where have you heard the word *representation*?

➡ What do you think *representation* means?

HOPE ACTIVITY

Now we are going to do an activity that shows us how we can find strength through hope. Can you help me answer some questions? Fill in the blanks for me:

When I turn on my television, I usually see Black or Hispanic people doing _____

_____.

I usually see Black or Hispanic people working _____

_____ types of jobs.

I *never* see Black or Hispanic people doing _____

_____.

I *never* see Black or Hispanic people working _____

_____ types of jobs.

Another adaptation is to display pictures with the question and have the students respond with their red, yellow, or green cards or use thumbs up, down, and sideways.

I am going to show you pictures (or words) on the screen that show different types of occupations. Have you ever seen a Black/Hispanic in person or on TV who is a

1. teacher,

2. astronaut,

3. professor,

4. chef,

5. rock star, or

6. police officer?

Think about the job you want to be when you grow up. Have you ever seen Black/Hispanic people in the job you want to do? Do

you think it will make it harder for you to be a(n)_____
_____ if you haven't seen a person like you doing that job?

If you've never seen a(n) _____
who is like you and you still plan to do whatever it takes to be a(n)
_____, then that means you have *hope*.

Hold up a picture of a mathematician and ask, "What do you think this person does for work?"

This person is a *mathematician*. Does anyone know what it means to be a mathematician? What kinds of jobs can mathematicians do?

- Have you ever seen a Black/Hispanic mathematician? Where?

- Do you see them very often? Why or why not?

- If Black and Hispanic children *never* or *rarely* see Black/Hispanic mathematicians, what might happen? They could think that it is impossible for a Black/Hispanic child to be a mathematician.

- Do you think that there are people who think it's impossible for Blacks/Hispanics to become mathematicians? Why or why not?

This lesson features *Hidden Figures: The True Story of Four Black Women and the Space Race* written by Margot Lee Shetterly with Winifred Conkling and illustrated by Laura Freeman. It is recommended for grades K–4. Guidelines are provided to support students at different levels of reading ability. Discussion questions will connect key concepts from the book to contemporary issues students may encounter in their homes and communities.

Look at the cover of the book *Hidden Figures: The True Story of Four Black Women and the Space Race.*

- What do you see on the cover?

- What do you think these women do?

They are mathematicians who helped the United States launch into outer space. At the time they became mathematicians, a lot of people thought it was *impossible*. So each of these women—Dorothy Vaughan, Mary Jackson, Katherine Johnson, and Christine Darden—had to have *hope* that their dream to be mathematicians would come true.

Read the story to your students, integrate student readers as appropriate, or access the following read-along option on the HarperKids YouTube channel.

We Grow Together

DISCUSSION QUESTIONS: HIDDEN FIGURES: THE TRUE STORY OF FOUR BLACK WOMEN AND THE SPACE RACE

➡ What were the main characters' names?

➡ Where did Dorothy Vaughan want to work?

➡ What was the problem at the beginning of the story?

➡ At the beginning of the story (during the 1940s), who were the computers?

➡ Why did some people think it was impossible for Dorothy to become a "computer"?

➡ What job did Mary Jackson want that others said was impossible?

➡ What stood in the way of Mary becoming an engineer?

➡ How did Mary respond to the obstacles in her way?

- ➡ What did Katherine Johnson want to do when others told her it was impossible? Why did they tell her it was impossible?

- ➡ Christine Darden started working in the "computer pool" many years after Dorothy, Mary, and Katherine had started. What was one reason that Christine felt confident she could do the job?

- ➡ Where did Dorothy, Mary, Katherine, and Christine work?

CLOSING REFLECTIONS

After reading *Hidden Figures: The True Story of Four Black Women and the Space Race*, we saw an example of how Dorothy, Mary, Katherine, and Christine had hope in so many ways. They had hope that their math skills would provide them the ability to achieve their dreams. They *persevered* even when it was really hard. They also helped *elevate* other women in the program by affirming their abilities and advocating for their right to be recognized and respected for their amazing skills.

Because they had hope for all that could be, not only were they engineers who could participate in their jobs just like Whites but they also made awesome contributions to the way we live now. Their work on planes changed lives and led to putting the first person on the moon.

They also opened the doors for so many other types of mathematicians. Did you know that it takes mathematicians to design video games? Did you know that the senior developer/designer for Xbox Kinect is a Black woman? Her name is Karisma Williams, and she continues to work at Microsoft developing and designing video games.

Lisette Titre-Montgomery, a successful art director, is another Black woman who has contributed to some of the industry's highest-profile games, including *Transformers: Age of Extinction*. Lisette also elevates students of color through her leadership role at

Gameheads. She was invited to work with President Obama's administration on ways to increase the opportunities for people of color in technology fields.

Now you know that it takes hope to achieve what some may say is impossible and that hope requires action—you have to make things happen. Now you also know that math is a part of the things we like to do too—like playing video games. Math can be fun.

We Strive Together

Lesson plans will include ELEVATE! Wise Words. The Wise Words vocabulary will be connected to the reading lesson designed to build language skills and help students meet Common Core benchmarks. Below, the focus is broken down by grade level.

"My son Michael loves the ELEVATE! program; he feels like they are family. Not only do I believe that the ELEVATE! program has sustained him academically but I also have seen an increase in his own confidence in his academic skills" (Michael Carter, ELEVATE! parent).

Kindergartners: With prompting and support, compare and contrast the adventures and experiences of characters in familiar stories, name the author and illustrator of a story and define the role of each in telling the story, describe the relationship between illustrations and the text in which they appear (e.g., what person, place, thing, or idea in the text an illustration depicts), and identify the reasons an author gives to support points in a text.[50]

First Graders: The goal for first graders is to use the illustrations and details in a text to describe its key ideas, identify the reasons an author gives to support points in a text, and identify basic similarities and differences between two texts on the same topic (e.g., in illustra-

---

50   Common Core State Standards Initiative, "English Language Arts Standards," accessed September 3, 2021, http://www.corestandards.org/ELA-Literacy/RL/K/.

tions, descriptions, or procedures). Additionally, encourage range of reading and level of text complexity with prompts and support for the student to read informational texts appropriately complex for grade 1 and encourage craft and structure knowledge through the identification of words and phrases in stories or poems that suggest feelings or appeal to the senses.[51]

"My son Michael loves the ELEVATE! program; he feels like they are family. Not only do I believe that the ELEVATE! program has sustained him academically but I also have seen an increase in his own confidence in his academic skills" (Michael Carter, ELEVATE! parent).

Second Graders: The goal is to describe how characters in a story respond to major events and challenges and identify the main purpose of a text, including what the author wants to answer, explain, or describe so that by the end of the year they can read and comprehend literature, including stories and poetry, in the grades 2–3 text complexity band proficiently, with scaffolding as needed at the high end of the range.[52]

Third Graders: The goal is to read with sufficient accuracy and fluency to support comprehension, read grade-level text with purpose and understanding, distinguish their own point of view from that of the narrator or of the characters, and determine the meaning of words and phrases as they are used in a text, distinguishing literal from nonliteral language.[53]

---

51   Ibid., accessed September 3, 2021, http://www.corestandards.org/ELA-Literacy/RL/1/.

52   Ibid., accessed September 3, 2021, http://www.corestandards.org/ELA-Literacy/RL/2/.

53   Ibid., accessed September 3, 2021, http://www.corestandards.org/ELA-Literacy/RL/3/.

WISE WORDS

General Vocabulary

➡ Hope

➡ Impossible

➡ Mathematician

➡ Obstacles

➡ Representation

➡ Dream

Hidden Figures Vocabulary

Grades K–1	Grades 2–3
Apart	Separate
Math	Computers
NASA	Americans
Space	Russia
	Laboratory
	Hidden Figures
	Aeronautics

We Work Together

This is where we allow students to expand the lesson beyond the book and apply other types of intelligence and experiences. This lesson's project demonstrates how we all use math throughout our day and is based on the following Common Core standards for math.

Kindergarten: Count to tell the number of objects. Understand the relationship between numbers and quantities; connect counting to cardinality.[54]

First Grade: Represent and solve problems involving addition and subtraction. Use addition and subtraction within 20 to solve word problems involving situations of adding to, taking from, putting together, taking apart, and comparing, with unknowns in all positions, e.g., by using objects, drawings, and equations with a symbol for the unknown number to represent the problem.[55]

Second Grade: Add and subtract within 20. Fluently add and subtract within 20 using mental strategies. By end of grade 2, know from memory all sums of two one-digit numbers.[56]

Third Grade: Represent and solve problems involving multiplication and division. Interpret products of whole numbers, e.g., interpret 5×7 as the total number of objects in 5 groups of 7 objects each. For example, describe a context in which a total number of objects can be expressed as $5 \times$.[57]

While students work on their projects, tap into one or more of the songs from ELEVATE!'s music library (https://app.sellwire. net/p/2GA) related to this lesson: "ELEVATE!," "ELEVATE! Affirmation," "ELEVATE! Superstars," "Children of Royalty," "When I Win, We Win," "Watch Me ELEVATE!," "It's Our Time," and "Elevating Hope."

MATERIALS

➡ Two large sugar cookies for each child.

---

54 Common Core State Standards Initiative, "Standards for Mathematical Practice," accessed September 3, 2021, https://ccss.math.content.k.cc.b.4.

55 Ibid., accessed September 3, 2021, https://ccss.math.content.1.oa.a.1.

56 Ibid., accessed September 3, 2021, https://ccss.math.content.2.oa.b.2.

57 Ibid., accessed September 3, 2021, https://ccss.math.content.3.oa.a.1.

➜ Filling: mix one part cream cheese to one part marshmallow crème (ensuring that there is sufficient mixture for each child to layer cream in between the cookies ½-inch thick).

➜ Rulers, sprinkles, plastic butter knife, paper bowl to hold the sprinkles, and plate for the final product.

INSTRUCTIONS

Each child should spread the cream mixture on one sugar cookie, about ½-inch thick. Then each child should put the remaining sugar cookie on top and then roll the side of the cookie in their sprinkles. Have students measure the height of their finished cookie sandwich and write down the measurement, then compare who has the thinnest and thickest.

COLLABORATIVE GROUP ACTIVITY

Welcome to the ELEVATE! Bakery. Imagine you are a baker and you own your own bakery. I'm going to ask you to cut your cookie into pieces so that you have more pieces to serve more customers.

Kindergarten: "ELEVATE! kindergarteners, cut your cookie into two pieces. If you have two pieces, how many cookies can you sell?" Then pair classmates together. "If two of you put your cookie pieces together, how many do you have in total?"

First Grade: "ELEVATE! first graders, please cut your cookie into four pieces. How many cookies can you sell if you have four pieces?" Then pair classmates together. "If you put your cookies together, how many can you sell? If you sell two cookies, how many do you have left? If you sell three cookies, how many do you have left? Okay, now I'm going to add another partner to your bakery. How many cookies do they have? Once you put your cookies together, how many do you have as a group? If you sell _____ cookies, how many do you now have left?"

Second Grade (and Late First Graders): Ask the group to cut pieces and then develop addition or subtraction problems that include adding and subtracting between group members. You can use the same process as for grade 1 using larger groups and more complex subtraction.

Third Grade: Develop questions that require students to double the number of pieces in their cookie or allow them to multiply/divide in larger quantities by placing them into groups. Pair up groups strategically so that you can ask questions like the following:

If group A has two cookies, and group B has six cookies, group B has _____ times more cookies than group A. That means group B can sell _____ times more cookies than group A.

If group B can sell _____times more cookies than group A, which group stands to make more money? It's not clear. Group B can sell more cookies, but they must divide the money by _____ number of people. If your group sells each cookie piece for $1, $2, $5, how much does the group make in sales as a whole? If the group has two, three, five members (etc.), how much will each group member make?

CONCLUSION

We learned a lot of important ways we depend on math—to build airplanes, put people into outer space, and build video games. We also use math to cook and sell food. The next time you hear someone say it's impossible for a Black person or *you* to be a mathematician, what will you say?

I will say, "Yes I can." We use math in everyday things like cooking and music. And I will say that hope is the way to achieve what people think is impossible. Look at Dorothy, Katherine, Mary, and Christine. If they could do it, so can I.

We Rise Together

This is the point where you and the students review the progress for the day or the week and reinforce the lessons and unit focus. It's time to lead them in affirming their progress!

"ELEVATE! SUPERSTARS"

➡ [Child's name, group name, or the entire class] is a superstar.

➡ [Child's achievement] makes [her/him/them] a superstar.

➡ Keep shooting for the stars.

➡ We love to watch you *elevate*!

Additional Resources

Songs from the ELEVATE! music library
(https://app.sellwire.net/p/2GA):

"ELEVATE!"

"ELEVATE! Affirmation"

"ELEVATE! Superstars"

"Children of Royalty"

"When I Win, We Win"

"Watch Me ELEVATE!"

"It's Our Time"

"Elevating Hope"

On the NASA.gov website, you will find the biographies of Mary W. Jackson, Katherine Johnson, Dorothy Vaughan, and Christine Darden.

CONCLUSION

WHAT WILL YOU DO to *elevate* Black student success?

I have heard the concerns of people who have struggled in this space. I did until I found success through the development and refining of Center of Hope's ELEVATE! curriculum. The ELEVATE! curriculum moves the discussion from failure to potential and hope for Black kids and elevates them from what they thought was impossible to possible, from what they thought they couldn't do to understanding that their potential has no limits, from believing they must express themselves the way society thinks they should to expressing themselves creatively and confidently for all to see.

Discovering this success with my students served to elevate my passion to find ways to replicate my success to influence more children. *Elevating Futures: A Model for Empowering Black Elementary Student Success* provides you the first step in answering the following:

- School administrators, how can you integrate ELEVATE!'s seven themes to elevate your school climate and the supplemental educational services in your building?

- Social service directors, how can you integrate ELEVATE!'s seven themes to elevate the quality of your after-school and prevention programs?

- Engagement teachers, how can you integrate ELEVATE!'s seven themes to elevate your classroom climate and teaching strategies to include student engagement, excitement, and real follow-through by students to complete their work?

- Parents and citizens, how can you, as a consumer, integrate ELEVATE!'s seven themes to elevate your advocacy for equity and quality programs in schools?

The twenty-eight lessons offered in my ELEVATE! curriculum guides will propel your school, classroom, and students on a holistic path of academic and social/emotional success. To receive my consultation services to assist in tailoring the skills and strategies in my curriculum guides to your individual classroom, school, and community, please contact me through https://doctor-p.com/book-us/.

GET IN TOUCH!

VISIT COHFS.ORG/CONSULTATION-SERVICES to learn more about workshops personal consultations and to inquire about speaking engagements.

Follow my social channels:

YouTube:
https://www.youtube.com/channel/
UCR38znqPmD6i5FgcSk2G0Gg

Twitter:
https://twitter.com/COHFSOrg

Facebook:
https://www.facebook.com/cohfs/

NOTES

CPSIA information can be obtained
at www.ICGtesting.com
Printed in the USA
BVHW041527020222
627891BV00002B/2

9 781642 252996